My Enemy,
My Brother

Also by Helen Heavirland

Zion, Champion for God

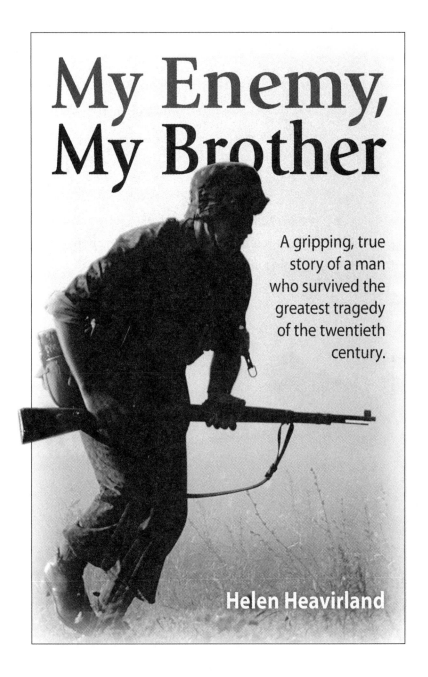

My Enemy, My Brother

A gripping, true
story of a man
who survived the
greatest tragedy
of the twentieth
century.

Helen Heavirland

Pacific Press® Publishing Association
Nampa, Idaho
Oshawa, Ontario, Canada
www.pacificpress.com

Cover design by Adam Jensen
Cover design resources from iStockphoto.com
Inside design by Steve Lanto
Inside photos supplied by the author

ISBN 13: 978-0-8163-2209-1
ISBN 10: 0-8163-2209-0

Additional copies of this book are available by calling toll-free
1-800-765-6955 or by visiting http://www.adventistbookcenter.com.

07 08 09 10 11 • 5 4 3 2 1

Dedication

To those who have felt the sting
of prejudice, betrayal, or guilt.

Contents

Preface

My Enemy, My Brother is not a political statement. It is simply the story of one man who survived one of the greatest tragedies of modern times and learned lessons valuable for all humanity in all times. It is not intended to be a precise history of events, but rather, it is Georg Grellmann's story as he observed and understood it from his time, place, and perspective.

In telling the story concisely, I have taken some liberties in re-creating conversations. For clarity, I have sometimes combined two or more people, events, or places into one. On occasion, a name has been provided or changed. The year noted with each chapter title corresponds with the beginning event of that chapter. Throughout, my goal has been to tell the truth clearly and, through this intriguing story, to bless readers with greater understanding of themselves and of others in their world.

When it was suggested that the story of Georg Grellman's early life be shared, he hesitated. "I rarely mentioned some of those years," he said. "I have noticed that often those in war who have seen the most, talk the least. I would be happy for the horrors never to come up again." In the end, he decided that if God could use his story to encourage someone else along a difficult way, it should be told. We hope this story will do just that.

—Helen Heavirland

CHAPTER 1

Wham!
1928

WHAM! Something whacked the back of my head.

I whirled around. A hand hit my mouth. My arms lifted to protect my face. A fist slugged me in the stomach. Gasping for breath, I felt myself falling backward. My head slammed against the cobblestone street.

"Whatcha doin' lyin' down, kid?" a tall boy taunted.

My head throbbed. Two boys stood over me, glaring down. They looked like giants.

"He's easy," the other boy sneered. "We can take him down anytime!"

I started to lift my head.

"Try getting up, and we'll knock you silly!" the first threatened.

My head dropped to the cobblestones again. My heart pounded in my throat. It seemed as though a lifetime passed until the older boys swaggered off, laughing.

What was that all about? I wondered as I lay there catching my breath. *I haven't done anything to them. I've never even seen them before.*

The boys finally disappeared. I sat up, glancing around nervously. My head felt strange. I picked up my first-grade arithmetic book and a pencil that had fallen out of the satchel over my shoulder. I got up, walked a few steps, then broke into a run—across the deserted market square, past the big Catholic church, past several apartment houses, alongside the prison. I crossed the street and bounded up the stairs of our apartment house.

Father was home when I dashed through the door. *If I tell what happened,* I thought, *Vater* [vaw´-ter] *will think* I *did something wrong.*

"Hello, Mutti [moo´-tee]," I greeted Mom, with the fond German term for mother. I made a beeline for the bedroom. My head hurt, but as usual I changed out of my school clothes and headed outside.

Three weeks earlier, my family had moved from the German village of Gornsdorf to the city of Gleiwitz. My sister, Hannchen (Hawn´-chin) was seven; I was six; my brother, Jo (Yo), was five.

Gornsdorf had felt safe. Hannchen and I had pulled a sled to the country to get milk, and no one bothered us. The only safety problem happened when we rode too fast on the way home, tipped over the sled in the snow, and got a milk bath!

Gornsdorf was small and quiet. I had loved exploring the hills and woods around the village. But the bustle of Gleiwitz intrigued me too. Every Friday, farmers brought produce to the market square at the end of our avenue. They parked their horse-drawn wagons up and down both sides of the cobblestone street. Hordes of customers went away with baskets overflowing with cabbage, potatoes, beans, beets, and turnips.

Every evening and morning the lamplighter rode his bicycle down the street, switching the lights on or off with his long stick, without even slowing down. Every day children played in the streets. Adults sauntered from one place to another. Horses clip-clopped along, pulling carts. Occasional black autos and trucks bounced through the streets, honking at whatever or whoever got in their way. Bicycles and their riders weaved in and out among the traffic.

Wham!

After school, between the traffic on my street, a dozen boys and girls usually played hide-and-seek or a ball game. It didn't take me long to get involved. Once I joined in the games, I soon got acquainted with our new neighbors.

Josel (Yo´-sul) was a regular at the after-school games. He was my age and lived on one of the upper floors in our apartment house. Even if there was no group game going, Josel and I could come up with some good or mischievous activity. We played together frequently.

Baerbel (Bar´-ble) also lived in our apartment house. She joined in the games and was a good runner. She was a year older than I, and taller. The morning after I got knocked down on my way home from school, Baerbel came down the stairs just as I headed out the door. "Where do you go to school?" she asked.

We figured out that her school was just beyond mine and headed off together, chattering all the way. I felt safer walking with her.

During school lunch break, an older boy picked up our ball and threw it hard toward the far end of the playfield. A boy in my class took off after it. The ball finally bounced a few times and then rolled to a stop. When my classmate was almost to the ball, two bigger boys ran toward him and jumped him.

"Ow!" he screamed, trying to protect himself with his arms. "Help!"

"Shut up, kid, or we'll *really* give you something to holler about!" an attacker snarled.

Both boys jabbed at him.

"Stop!" my classmate screamed. "Leave me alone!"

The older boys knocked him down, kicked him a couple times, and then walked off, laughing.

I stood, frozen. He hadn't done anything to them. *Like yesterday afternoon,* I thought.

"When I'm big enough," a boy near me growled, "I'll get them."

As the weeks passed, every now and again I saw scuffles. I began to notice a pattern. Whether on the playground or walking to or from school, I watched for would-be attackers. No one ever jumped me when Baerbel and I walked together.

My problems didn't stop with fights. The first half of my first-grade year we were still living in Gornsdorf. School was great fun—most of the time we played games outside. For a little while each school day, we drew lines and circles with slate pencils. But when we moved to the city, I found that my classmates could write simple sentences and add and subtract numbers. My face flushed with embarrassment—I knew no letters or numbers. I didn't understand what the teacher was trying to teach us. I carried my pencils and books home as the teacher instructed, but I couldn't read them at home any better than I could at school.

Christmas break felt like escape—no reading or writing or numbers I couldn't fathom, jumping all over in my head. I could still play outside with Josel and Baerbel and the other kids from the apartment houses—when it wasn't so bitterly cold that we couldn't stand to be out in it.

For Christmas celebration, Mutti burned spruce needles for fragrance. She decorated the house with a few evergreen twigs. Each year we received practical gifts—shoes, underwear, or other clothes—and always one toy. One Christmas back in Gornsdorf, Vater had built a little grocery store for me. It had a balance scales with weights from one to ten grams. I filled the tiny drawers with sugar, flour, salt, rice, and whatever else Mutti allowed. That same Christmas, Vater built a dollhouse for Hannchen. Jo received a beautiful electric train. He enjoyed the train so much that he hardly had time to play with the second toy he got for the same Christmas—a Merklin building set.

Much too soon, Christmas break was over, and I had to go back and sit in a classroom while the teacher talked about stuff I didn't understand. Occasionally on the way home various bullies still jumped me. One afternoon Mutti took a second look at me when I arrived home from school. She took my face in her hands and looked at the sore spot under my left eye. "How'd you get this scrape, Georg?"

I swallowed hard and looked down at the floor. "Two boys hit me on the way home from school."

"Did you do anything mean to those boys?" she questioned.

"No. I didn't even see them coming."

"Is this the first time that's happened?"

I shook my head. "No." I swallowed hard, but the story tumbled out—the shock of the first time, watching and avoiding being in the empty market square by myself, the fights on the playground.

"Who fights?" Mutti asked.

"The k-k-kids from school," I stammered. "The Catholics take up most the school, and there are just a few rooms at one end for the Protestants. They fight with each other."

Mutti washed the wound and spread a homemade salve on it. She sighed. Her eyes darkened. Finally she looked me in the eye and said, "I'm afraid it's time you learn a new word."

CHAPTER 2

A New Word
1929

"What new word?" I asked.

"*Das V—*" Mutti stopped and cocked her head as she thought. "Just a minute. First, tell me, who are your friends that you play with out in the street after school?"

"Josel and Baerbel and Henri and . . ." I listed the regulars.

"And you have lots of fun with them. Right?"

"*Ja* [yaw]!" I exclaimed.

"Are any of them from Gornsdorf, where we moved from?" Mutti asked.

"No."

"How many of them go to the same church we go to?"

"None of them."

"Are any of their fathers pastors?"

"No . . . well, Josel's. Isn't a rabbi like a pastor?"

"*Ja,*" Mutti agreed. "There are lots of differences among

1929 or 1930—Georg at seven or eight years old, while living in Gleiwitz. L to R, Mutti, Hannchen, Jo (Joachim), Georg, Vater

your friends. Josel is Jewish, Baerbel is Catholic, and we're Protestant. Most of them are probably German, but Henri is from Poland. And you have fun with them all. Right?"

"*Ja.*"

"You all get along fine here in front of our apartment house," Mutti said. "Why do children from those same groups fight at school?"

I shrugged my shoulders. "I don't know."

"The new word I mentioned," Mutti continued, "is *das Vorurteil* [prejudice]."

I waited for her to explain.

"Prejudice is the attitude of people who treat others badly just because they are different."

"Huh?"

Mutti's eyebrows scrunched closer together. "Well . . ." she started, and then stopped. Her eyes seemed to look at someplace far away. After a moment, she looked back at me. "Prejudice is about more than differences," she said. "It's about meanness in a person's heart. God wants to put love in our hearts, so we will treat everyone with respect."

As the weeks passed, I got beaten up a few more times, but I never was attacked when, on the way to my school, I accompanied Baerbel as she walked to the Catholic portion of the girls' school.

When our family had first moved to Gleiwitz, Hannchen was behind in school too. A tutor helped her every day after school until she caught up with her classmates. I didn't get any help with my schoolwork. At the end of the school year, I overheard Vater talking about me.

"*Ja, fressen kann er, nur nicht lernen* [He can eat but not learn]."

I felt humiliated. *Fressen* was a word used only for animals.

The new school year started in spring, shortly after Easter. I hung my head when I walked into first grade—again. I was taller than everyone else in the class. The second-grade boys teased me.

As for schoolwork, it helped to start at the beginning. Letters and numbers made sense. Learning was fun. But, even though I was often at the top in my class, my favorite times were after school, weekends, and summers.

Sometimes our family went for walks in the woods near the city, discovering new birds or bugs. We kids liked rolling down a grassy hillside and feeling the breeze mussing our hair and cooling the sun's rays. Sometimes we watched the sun go down, listened to the frogs start their night songs, and watched for the first stars.

"There's the Big Dipper!"

"There's Orion!"

"There's the North Star!"

Heading into the mountains or heading back home, I almost always led the way.

"You just seem to know what direction to go," Mutti often said.

Occasionally we rode our bicycles into the country and picnicked at some spot that caught our fancy. In winter we ice-skated together at a pond near the city.

I enjoyed the time outside with my family. I also liked the stillness when I got to explore by myself. Sometimes in summer, Vater would let me ride my bicycle ten miles west to a farm belonging to some members of our church—the Hassa family. I loved riding my bicycle through fields and hills, smelling the fresh country fragrances and feeling the breeze on my face—and I liked the warm welcome when I arrived. Frau Hassa's eyes always danced.

"Welcome! Welcome!" she would gush in Polish. "Are you hungry?" At the least, she or one of their two girls would get me a cup of cold water, fresh from the spring. When Frau Hassa couldn't find the right German word, Herr Hassa or one of the girls translated into their broken German—with a Polish accent.

The Hassa family welcomed me to do whatever they were doing. I fed the cow, turned the cream separator, and churned butter. Then I got to drink all I wanted of the fresh buttermilk with small pieces of butter in it.

When night arrived, I curled up in the soft straw in the barn's hayloft, feeling appreciated and content. It made no difference that our native languages were different. I breathed deeply the scent of clean straw and listened to the cow chewing her cud below. What a treat for a country-loving city boy!

At home one winter morning, I wakened early. Dawn had started to lighten the sky. I got up and looked out the window. The moon's big, orange ball tempted me to go out and experience the wonder. I got dressed, tiptoed out of the bedroom, grabbed my winter coat, and slipped out the apartment door.

My breath puffed into little white clouds under the street lamps. I wandered through the streets and then beyond city apartments and lights. About sunrise, I ended up at a country pond—not a house in sight. I threw stones onto the ice. It held. I stepped onto it gingerly. Not a sound. I walked across the pond. No creaking or cracking. I ran and slid, ran and slid, squealing with delight. Suddenly, I heard an eerie *cr-r-ee-ee-ea-k*. In the same second, the ice fell out from under me.

Icy water closed in around me. My lungs burned. They felt as though they might explode. My arms flailed. Why hadn't I learned to swim?

Finally I surfaced, coughing and gasping.

I grabbed the ice and then stretched my arms as far as I could reach over the frozen surface and pushed down gently. The ice broke. Over and over, it dropped me back into freezing water. I felt that I didn't have the strength to lift my arms again.

But what choice do I have?

I forced myself to lift my arms onto the ice again. I pushed down. Crack. I plummeted again. My waterlogged coat held me down—it seemed like forever before I surfaced again, coughing and spluttering.

Will Mutti and Vater ever know what happened to me? I wondered.

I lifted my arms onto the ice again. Using just enough weight to keep me from sinking but not enough to break the ice, I rested a moment. My teeth chattered.

I pushed against the ice with all the energy I could muster. It broke—but not quite as quickly. Again. The ice closer to shore was thicker. Finally it held, but I didn't have the strength to propel myself onto it.

I rested again and then tried again. I kicked my feet. I pushed with my elbows. I clawed with my fingers. My shoulders rose. I lay with my chest down on the ice.

I rested a moment and then tried again. Slowly I raised my legs and then stretched out flat and rolled toward the bank. At the edge, I lay shivering. My breaths came fast and shallow. *I've got to get home,* I thought. I sat up, sucked in a few more breaths, and then stood. Forcing one foot in front of the other, I took a step, then another step, and another. I sped up till I was running toward home.

Not sure what would happen if my adventure was discovered, I snuck into our apartment, found dry clothes, and changed in the bathroom. I was still shivering when Mutti called, "Breakfast." That morning, the hot potatoes felt really good!

The next time Vater read from Psalm 34, verse 7 caught my attention. "The angel of the Lord encampeth round about them that fear him, and delivereth them."

Was it my guardian angel who gave me the energy to keep trying to get out of the icy pond? I wondered. *Could God possibly care about one kid? About me?*

Powers
1930

One Sunday afternoon I was at home in the backyard when I heard shouting—not the happy shrieks of kids playing ball or the insistent shouts of parents calling children. I hurried around the apartment house and onto the front sidewalk to see what was happening. A moment later Hannchen and Jo joined me.

A sea of people surged down the street toward us. Red flags waved above them. Men punched the air with their fists in rhythm with angry shouts.

My heart beat faster.

The bedroom window above us screeched open, and Mutti stuck her head out. She looked up and down the street. When she saw the mob, her face turned white. "Children," she commanded, "come in at once!"

Mutti met us at the door. She and Vater joined us at the bedroom window. The mob drew closer, filling the whole street.

"What a lot of people!" Jo said.

"How many are there?" Hannchen asked.

Vater surveyed the crowd. "There must be four or five hundred."

"Arbeiter der Welt erhebt euch!" the mob shouted. "Workers of the world arise!" "Workers unite!" Among the red flags, an army of fists

jabbed at the sky. The shouting and stamping of feet reverberated between our apartment house and the brick prison across the street.

A shiver went down my spine. "What are they doing?" I asked.

The question hung in the air unanswered. Finally Vater spoke. "I don't really know," he admitted. "But it must have something to do with politics."

A minute later Mutti asked, "Isn't a new political party using red flags?"

"Ja," Vater answered. "The Communist Party."

Mutti looked from the window, toward Vater. "Aren't they the ones who—" She stopped midsentence.

I looked up from the window. Mutti and Vater gave each other one of those looks that happened when they knew more than they were going to tell us.

"The ones who what?" I asked.

"Oh, nothing," Mutti said.

I looked out the window again. The mob had stopped and turned toward the prison across the street. The shouting quieted, and then it started again with new words. "They're yelling something different," I said.

It started out quieter than before but got louder than ever. "Let them out! Let them out!"

"What's it mean?" I asked.

"Some of the Communist Party members were arrested and put in prison," Vater said.

"Why?"

Mutti gave Vater one of her looks. "Come, everyone," she said. "Let's go read a story."

"Good idea," Vater agreed. "These people are probably just demonstrating." He headed into the living room.

I followed, asking, "What's den-us-bra . . ."

"Demonstrating," Hannchen corrected.

"Yeah, well, what is it?"

"They're probably just trying to get attention," Vater said. "Probably trying to scare the government leaders and get them to do what they want."

Mutti pulled a book out of the bookcase. "Want a *Lebensbilder* story?" she asked.

"*Ja,*" we chorused.

We loved stories. Most evenings at bedtime Mutti called, "Story time." She pulled out one of the *Life Builder* books—a set of children's books full of true stories. Hannchen, Jo, and I vied for the best position. As always, when Mutti suggested extra stories, we gathered round quickly.

The stories calmed us. Finally, at suppertime, the demonstration broke up and the street was quiet again.

"There is one thing we have not had to worry about since we have lived here in Gleiwitz," Mutti said. "Remember the oppressive atmosphere that came over our apartment house in Gornsdorf sometimes?"

"*Ja,*" I agreed. "When you sent me to the cellar to get a bucket of coal or potatoes, a spooky feeling chased me down the stairs. Even when the temperature was hot, the eerie feeling made me shiver."

"And sometimes we couldn't sleep," Hannchen added, "because, after the lights were turned off, little black beings flitted all over our room. I *hated* it when they came into our beds. 'Mutti, Mutti!' we called."

Shivers went down my spine. "When you came and turned on the light," I added, "the little black beings disappeared. You would calm us and then go back to your own bed. But after you turned the lights off and left, the black beings came back."

"Yes," Mutti said. "One evening when Vater was gone and you children were in bed, I sat in a chair in the living room, reading my Bible. Suddenly it lifted off my knees, flew against the wall in the far corner of the room, and fell to the floor."

"It took a while," Vater added, "for us to figure out that the eerie times coincided with séances held by the neighbors in the apartment above us. After that, when you children got nervous about little black beings in your room, we took you all into bed with us."

"Remember the night when Vater was gone?" Hannchen asked. "And we were all in bed with Mutti while she read stories till Vater came home?"

I remembered that evening. We pulled the quilt to our chins and snuggled up close to Mutti, partly to see the pictures, partly to feel her comfort. She read us story after story. Still, we were wide awake.

Close to midnight Vater arrived. He had just joined us in bed when we all heard a knock outside the bedroom window. He got up and checked. Nobody was there. He came back to bed. A knock came at the kitchen window. Again, he got up and checked. Again, nobody. But as soon as he was in bed, the knock came again. We children held our breath.

Vater tapped on the bed frame with different timing than the earlier knocking. At the bedroom window, the knocking came again— with the exact timing of Vater's taps. Vater tapped again with changed tempo. The new tap and tempo was repeated on the window. Vater spoke clearly and firmly, "I know who you are, devil."

More knocking came. Vater ignored it. "Let me tell you a story," he said. "Not long after Mutti and I got married, when I was first a pastor, a famous spiritualist medium went from city to city performing many miracles. Sometimes he invited a woman in his audience to come onto the stage. He hypnotized the woman, gave her a baby bottle, and instructed her to suck on it. Then he brought her back to consciousness while she was still sucking on the bottle. Blushing, the woman ran from the stage while the audience laughed.

"At one of this medium's performances, he invited anyone who would like to, to come up to the stage and think something but not say what he thought. The spiritualist said, 'Then I'll act out what you thought.'

"A man came forward. The medium took his hand. He led the

volunteer outside and through the city streets. The audience followed, causing quite a commotion.

"The spiritualist stopped in front of a tobacco store. He, the volunteer, and as many others as could, crowded into the store. The proprietor looked up, shocked at the crowd. The spiritualist walked behind the counter, reached up to the top shelf, took down a specific box, opened it, picked up a particular brand of cigar, and handed it to the man. 'Is that what you were thinking?' he asked.

" *'Ja-a-a,'* the man stuttered."

Vater took a deep breath.

"Can the devil read our thoughts?" I asked.

"No," Mutti answered, "not unless we open ourselves up to him. But when this man went to see the spiritualist and when he offered to be part of the demonstration, he opened himself up to the devil. Do you understand?"

"He chose the devil rather than Jesus?" I asked.

"Ja."

Vater continued. "Wherever this spiritualist advertised, crowds flocked to his meetings. One day I saw his advertisement for coming to our town. At home I paced back and forth. 'We know what this man does!' I told Mutti. 'We know the powers behind it. Yet we do nothing.'

" 'What can we do?' she asked.

"An idea came to me. I talked to the church leaders. We rented the city hall and advertised our own meeting. We invited the spiritualist and promised to disclose the power behind his performances.

"The next few days, the whole town was stirred up. The night of our meeting, so many people crowded into the hall that the police came to try to keep order, just in case there was a problem. Half of our church members were there, acting as ushers.

"When I stepped onto the platform, I saw men and women sitting all across the front rows with their arms linked together . . . like this." Vater pulled Jo's arm through his at the elbow to demonstrate.

"Some of the people with their arms linked together had a strange, evil look on their faces. Their heads jerked. I didn't see the spiritualist himself, but I was sure he'd sent these men and women.

"At first I was frightened. *Will all these people try to surround me?* I wondered. *What will they do to me?*

"I opened my mouth to speak, but no sound came out. I looked down at the podium and swallowed. I opened my mouth again but couldn't say a word. It felt as if something very powerful was holding my tongue.

"The group with their arms linked glared at me. I'd never seen such evil eyes."

Vater stopped talking. He took a couple of deep breaths.

"Then I remembered," Vater continued. "I remembered the other half of our church members. They weren't at this meeting. They were at our church building . . . and they were praying. They would be there throughout this meeting, praying."

Vater's voice changed as he told us the story. "Remember the Bible story about when Jesus cast the demons out of the men that lived in the graveyard?"

"Ja, ja," we children chorused.

"There in city hall," Vater continued, "I remembered that half of our church members were praying to the God who cast out those evil spirits.

"Silently, I prayed again, 'God, I'm no match for the evil that's here before me. But You are! Again, I ask You to cleanse me from all unrighteousness. And I ask You, in the name of Jesus Christ, to show Your power . . . for Your glory.'

"I took a deep breath. 'Tonight,' I said in a strong, clear voice, 'we've come to talk about power.'

"As soon as I started speaking, a look of shock came over the faces of the people in the front rows.

"I told the crowd about a good God and an evil devil. The people in the front rows glared at me. But they sat still and stayed quiet. I spoke freely throughout the evening about which was the greater power.

"The next evening our whole church met to pray again—to praise God for what He had done.

"Later we were told about the spiritualist's next meeting. He stepped confidently onto the platform, but he was unable to perform his magic. After several attempts, he apologized. 'There is a superior power preventing this program,' he said.

"After those two meetings, many people requested Bible studies. Some of the studies were in the homes of spiritualists. I learned always to take another person along to pray while I studied with them.

"Word traveled around the country. The spiritualist never regained his former influence.

"It was that same power," Vater said, "that was upstairs in those séances. He wanted to be in our apartment too. But God is stronger. Do you hear the knocking anymore?"

We had listened in silence. "No," Hannchen said.

"It faded away," I added, "shortly after you started the story."

"The devil is strong," Vater said. "And he is our enemy. But *always* remember this—God is much, much stronger."

After a moment of silence, Mutti had thrown back the covers. "Off to bed, dear children."

Heading back to my bed wasn't hard after Vater's story. I crawled in, pulled the quilt up to my chin, and felt cozy as I reminded myself, *God is much, much stronger.* I didn't think I'd ever forget that.

CHAPTER 4

I Won't Waste Money on You
1931

One afternoon while Vater was gone across the city to visit people from church, I heard a dull roar down the street again. Over the last few months, various groups had demonstrated in different locations all over the city. The crowds of marchers had gotten larger. Usually the demonstrations in our street were peaceful, but when other groups held opposing demonstrations, scuffles sometimes broke out. The prison across the street from our apartment house became the scene of more and more frequent demonstrations. But this time it was unusually loud.

I looked down the street and saw red flags waving. Feet pounded. Fists punched the air. Even women and children screamed along with the men.

Neighbors up and down the street—children, teens, women, men—hurried inside. I grabbed my bicycle and carried it up the steps into our apartment house.

Mutti met me at our door and locked it behind me.

The noise got louder and louder as the Communist demonstrators approached. "Workers of the world, unite!" the marchers screamed, their fists punctuating each pronouncement. "Workers of the world, unite!"

I rolled my bicycle into the bedroom.

"Workers of the world, unite! Workers of the world, unite!"

I looked out the window at what looked like a sea of red flags. The chants were almost deafening. I looked down the street. I'd never seen a demonstration stretch so far.

The bedroom door creaked. Mutti joined me at the window.

"It's the biggest group of demonstrators I've ever seen," I said.

Mutti looked down the street. "There are lots this time," she observed.

"There must be twice as many people as last time," I said. "And that time Vater said there must have been more than a thousand people."

"So," Mutti asked, "if there were a thousand last time and there are twice as many this time, how many are out there now?"

"Two thousand," I answered.

Mutti smiled down at me. "I'm glad you like mathematics," she said. She tousled my hair and then stepped away from the window. "Come help in the kitchen," she said.

I followed Mutti as the mob continued screaming, "Workers of the world, unite! Workers of the world, unite!"

"Hannchen, Jo," Mutti called on the way through the living room, "come help."

We washed and dried lunch dishes together.

"Mutti," I asked as I dried a plate, "why do all these people march and scream?"

Mutti was quiet a moment, as though she was thinking. "They want all the workers to make enough money so they can take care of their families and have enough food for them," she said.

"Don't people earn money when they work?" I asked.

"Yes," Mutti said, "but some people have lots of money and some have just a little. These people want the rich people to help the poor people."

"Isn't that good?"

"Yes," Mutti answered. "It's good to share."

"Are there hungry people?" I persisted.

"I'm sure there are some hungry people."

"Will these demonstrations help?"

"Georg, Georg," Mutti said. "You have a curious mind. That's good. But you have more questions than I have answers. I really don't keep up with politics very well. I don't know if they can help. Let's think about something else for a while."

The chanting outside changed as the demonstrators gathered around the prison. "Let them out! Let them out!"

Mutti grabbed a pan of beets and one of rutabagas she'd brought in earlier from the garden. "We need to clean these for supper," she said.

As we started cleaning vegetables, Mutti's eyes brightened. "Let's say some of the Bible verses we've memorized." She started, " 'The angel of the Lord . . .' "

We all chimed in, " '. . . encampeth round about them that fear him, and delivereth them,' " we chorused. "Psalm thirty-four, verse seven."

"Psalm ninety-one, verse fifteen," Hannchen suggested.

Together we repeated the verse. " 'He shall call upon me, and I will answer him: I will be with him in trouble; I will deliver him, and honour him.' "

"And verse five," I suggested.

" 'Thou shalt not be afraid for the terror by night; nor for the arrow that flieth by day.' "

"Psalm twenty-three," Jo offered.

Together we repeated the psalm.

"Tell us a story," I suggested.

"Ja! Ja!" Hannchen and Jo agreed.

So, Mutti told us stories while we worked and then read us stories while supper cooked.

The din outside died down about sunset. Vater made it home in time to eat supper with us.

*   *   *

When I was ready for middle school, tuition cost ten marks per month for boys—ten marks in the German currency equaled about four United States dollars. Vater paid the fees. I started classes.

Algebra was fun. Science intrigued me. History fascinated me. Geography helped make history come alive. Then there was language.

In the first French class, the teacher bragged and boasted and crowed about his experience as an officer in World War I. He didn't say anything about his qualifications for teaching French. After introducing himself, the French "teacher" barked, "You will each introduce yourself. When I come to you, stand up, look me in the eye, and state your last name clearly. You may be seated when I move on to another student."

One by one the students stood, gave their names, and the "teacher" repeated each. When he came to me, I stood and stated clearly, "Grellmann."

The teacher's eyes narrowed. The edges of his mouth turned up in an evil-looking grin. He sneered, "Master Bettelmann it shall be."

From then on he called me Bettelmann, which means beggar man. Every time he did, irritation threatened to explode inside me. I hadn't done anything wrong. Why would he ridicule me? Knowing I could easily get myself in trouble, I clamped my mouth shut.

Day after day, Herr "Colonel of the French Class" smelled of liquor. Though smoking was *verboten* (forbidden) in any classroom, the French "teacher" smoked openly. It seemed as though he blew smoke especially toward those students who most disliked him. I despised him so much that I hated even to think about French.

When Vater saw my first report card, he snapped, "I won't waste money on you. You can go back to elementary school."

Mutti pleaded my case. Vater gave me "the look." "Come with me," he said.

"But Va—"

"Come."

He marched to the middle school and into my main teacher's room. I plodded along behind.

"Herr Bruchmann, I've come to get Georg's papers so he can go back to elementary school."

Herr Bruchmann's smile disappeared. "Good afternoon, Herr Grellmann," he said tentatively. "How can I help you?"

There was no smile in Vater's voice. "Give me Georg's papers, please."

Herr Bruchmann looked at me. I hung my head. He looked back up to Vater. "You can't be serious."

"I am totally serious. I won't waste money on a child who won't learn."

"But, Herr Grellmann, Georg is doing well in school. He has high marks in every class . . . except French. But most students did even worse in French. And their parents aren't putting them back in elementary school."

"Give me his records, please."

"Herr Grellmann," my teacher pleaded, "Georg is an excellent student. He is capable. He's—"

Vater held out his hand. "His records?"

Chapter 5

Inevitable
1933

Elementary school was inevitable. I tried to make the best of it. I avoided fights when I could. As I grew taller, fewer bullies attacked. Besides, the more adept I became at defending myself, the less desirable I was as a target.

When I was eleven, the Nazi party leader, Adolf Hitler, became chancellor of Germany. Over the next couple of years I occasionally heard my parents or others talk about how glad they were that the Nazi party rather than the Communist Party had gained leadership in the country. They discussed the fact that unemployment was decreasing and the economy improving. It must have been so. More often than he used to, Vater brought home a chocolate bar and divided it among our family members.

From time to time I overheard snatches of adult conversations about fighting—between Catholics and Protestants, Jews and Gentiles, Germans and Poles. And between members of the Communist Party and members of the *Nationalsozialistiche Deutsche Arbeiterpartei*—the National Socialist German Worker's party, more commonly known as the Nazi party.

When I was thirteen, our family moved from Gleiwitz, near the Polish border, to Breslau, the beautiful capital city of the state of Silesia. It

35

was also the seventh largest city in Germany. We moved into a second-floor apartment on a wide street. Two lanes of traffic ran east and two ran west. In the center, tram-car lines ran in both directions. As in Gleiwitz, the most common mode of transportation was bicycles.

Going to elementary school again disappointed me. If I didn't go through middle school, I couldn't go on to *gymnasium*—boys' high school. Without a high school diploma I could never attend a university. I'd never be able to enter a profession. The one thing I wanted to do, I never could do. I tried not to think about it—just buried myself in what I could do.

The history teacher was an enthusiastic man who made his subject intriguing. He explained how German history fit into world history. We learned about various wars in past centuries that took land from Germany and the battles in which Germany fought back and reclaimed German soil and peoples.

History class got even more interesting when our patriotic teacher started talking about the current century. We learned that France had tried to surround Germany—some of France's military alliances at the beginning of World War I were with Russia, Romania, Serbia, Italy, and a secret alliance with England. Then Austria's crown prince was murdered on a visit to Sarajevo in Serbia. Austria wanted justice, demanding that the murderers be handed over. Serbia conferred with France, then France with her other allies. Word was sent back to Serbia that if Austria sent troops into Serbia, the troops of France and her allies would march to Serbia's defense. Serbia's protecting the murderers provoked Austria to declare war. Since Austria had an alliance with Germany, our country, too, was dragged into what became World War I.

We learned that the settlement after World War I had given German land to surrounding nations, including France, Poland, and Denmark; that all of Germany's former colonies in Africa and in the Pacific Islands were taken away from us; that we had to surrender all gold reserves and pay reparations to other countries, so that Germany as a country went bankrupt. After the war, the people of Germany were so poor that many thousands starved to death.

After the class on the German economy after World War I, I went home and found Mutti in the kitchen. "Were you poor after World War I?" I asked.

Mutti closed her eyes and took a deep breath. She looked sad. She opened her eyes and looked straight into mine. "*Everyone* in Germany was poor," she said. "Hardly anybody had work."

"But Vater did, didn't he?"

"After Vater got out of school, he had work, but sometimes he didn't get paid much. And sometimes he didn't get paid on time."

"Did you always have food?"

"God always provided something for us to eat," Mutti replied, "but sometimes we didn't have very much. And sometimes all we had for days on end was potatoes, potatoes, potatoes." She sighed. "But that was more than a lot of people had.

"Even potatoes were precious," she continued. "For Christmas one year, some people received the gift of one potato. And they were thankful for it! Sometimes when Vater would go out to a farmer and give a Bible study, he might come home with a bit of food, but sometimes he came away with nothing."

Mutti stirred the pot of soup on the stove. "I'm just thankful you kids are all healthy." She turned toward me and smiled. "I'm thankful it's so-o-o much better now! It's still hard to make ends meet sometimes," she said, "but have you been hungry when you went away from the table anytime lately?"

"No. Not after a meal," I said. "But I'm hungry now."

"As fast as you're growing, I'm not surprised!" Mutti grinned. "Go change out of your school clothes," she added. "Supper will be on the table in no time."

Besides history, math class was my favorite. I shared a bench with Kaul. He was better in composition than I, and I was better in math. We helped each other.

Kaul helped me in another way too. Since I didn't go to school on Saturdays, on Sunday morning I visited Kaul to get the assignments so I could be ready for Monday morning.

When Kaul wasn't available, I got the assignments from another classmate. He was the leader of one of the local Hitler Youth groups. He encouraged me to join. He didn't pressure me directly, but in the end I joined, along with the rest of my classmates.

During break one day, I went with a couple of other boys in my class to investigate the basement of our school. We knew it was off limits, but we were curious. It housed a heating system with big pipes and other equipment. We also discovered an underground extension that led to the girls' school.

When our break was about over, we headed back. Suddenly we heard footsteps coming down a staircase.

The other boys' eyes got big. My heart pounded in my throat. I noticed a fire hose lying on the floor. "Open the hydrant!" I ordered.

Water shot like a cannon at the door just as it opened. The teacher of our next class, who was also the school principal, got the full force. Quickly he pulled the door closed.

We turned off the water and ran up a different stairway to the second floor to our classroom. We scooted into our seats, trying to look nonchalant.

Our principal entered the classroom. His shoes sloshed with each step. His shirt and pants were soaked. His hair hung wet. "Who was down in the basement?" he asked.

The room was silent.

He waited at the head of the class.

Nobody said a word.

Again he asked, "Who was down in the basement?"

Since I sat in the front row, I thought he could hear my heart thumping. I stood up. Then I looked behind me to share the blame.

No one else stood.

I looked toward the front again. I couldn't read the expression on the principal's face. My face felt hot. The silence in the room seemed ready to explode.

After what seemed like forever, the principal said, "You may be seated, Georg."

I sat down, heart still pounding.

He went on with class as if nothing had happened.

After school, I cornered my buddies-in-crime: "Some friends you are!" I snapped. "It wasn't fair for you to let me take all the blame!"

"He didn't do anything to you," one said.

"Nothing's going to happen," the other added. "He likes you."

I wasn't sure he liked me well enough to let our prank go by. But days passed with no repercussions.

As spring approached, Mutti asked Vater repeatedly, "What will we do for a garden?" Our brick apartment house in Breslau was squeezed in among others. None of them had garden plots. At first, some church friends a few blocks away shared their small plot with us. Eventually, Vater discovered a space for rent, but it was three miles away across the city.

Since I was stronger than either my brother or sister, Mutti often asked me to help with the gardening. I liked eating, and I liked Mutti; so, I helped—usually without complaint. I wasn't fond of the job, but it needed to be done. Before long, watering became my responsibility.

I rode my bicycle to the garden carrying two empty buckets and then hauled water from the hand pump to our garden—about two hundred yards. Each watering took twelve to fifteen trips with both buckets full. With each bucket of water, I disliked gardening a little more.

Some Sundays Herbert, a friend from church, came along and helped. If I got done sooner, we had more time for adventure—like going for a swim or cycling to the Zopten, a mountain about twenty-five miles from town.

During the week, school came before adventure. Even before gardening.

One morning when I left our apartment house to go to school, a heavy truck with huge wheels was parked across the street. Just as a man on a bicycle passed the truck, a heavy spring on the outside of the truck's wheels came loose. Under enormous tension, it swirled through the air toward the man on the bicycle. In a split-second, the bicycle slid across the street. Something flew off to the side. The man screamed a blood-curdling scream. He flew through the air and landed, sprawled on the pavement, wailing.

Something looked wrong with the way he was lying on the ground. He had two arms . . . but only one leg. A man came running with the thing that had flown off to the side. A shoe was on one end. "His leg!" he shouted. "His leg!"

My heart beat so hard it felt as though it might jump out of my chest. Men and women came running and surrounded the man. Even with his screams, I heard the cacophony of people trying to help. Shortly, an ambulance arrived.

I headed toward school. But the ambulance's leaving didn't erase the man's screams from my mind. It was the most pain-filled, the most horrendous, the most desperate sound I'd ever heard. I couldn't stop thinking about the man on the bicycle—one moment he was fine; the next his whole world had changed. I thought of myself—I'd hate not being able to run, to hike, to climb mountains, to ride my bicycle into the country.

Without one of his legs, the man would be limited in what he could do. *In a way,* I thought, *like I will be limited . . . because I've lost my chance to go to gymnasium* [high school] *and university.*

I was nearly through with elementary school. What was I going to do? What would Vater have in mind for me?

*   *   *

When my brother Jo had finished fourth grade, he went to middle school and then later to *gymnasium,* at a cost of fifteen marks per month. His first report card showed he had done worse in Hebrew

40

and in Greek than I had done in French when Vater had put me back in elementary school.

Vater looked over Jo's report card. "You'll work on the language grades, won't you?"

"*Ja,*" Jo responded casually.

"Good," Vater said. He handed Jo's report card to him and went back to reading a book.

Jo went to change clothes.

Something inside me hurt in a way I couldn't identify. *Why is it OK for Jo to get poor grades but not for me?*

A few evenings later, Vater called me to sit down with him in the living room. "Your mother and I have been talking," he said. "You're fourteen and you're almost through with school. It's time to think about what you're going to do with your life."

I had known this discussion would be coming sometime soon.

"We've thought and thought about what you'd be good at," he said. "Then we came up with the perfect solution."

My mind rumbled on ahead, trying to figure out what kind of a job Vater thought I'd do well.

He smiled. "You could be a very good gardener."

CHAPTER 6

Stuck
1937

Gardener! my mind screamed. My head felt as if it were swirling. I took a deep breath. "N-n-no," I stammered.

Vater's smile disappeared.

"I don't want to be a gardener," I said. "I want to be a dentist."

Vater cleared his throat. "I see you have done some thinking about it."

"*Ja,* Vater. That's what I want to do."

"But, how can you?" he asked.

There were two kinds of dentists. Some received a doctorate from the university. They could perform surgical procedures. Other dentists could do only dentures, crowns, bridges, fillings, and extractions. Their minimum education usually was middle school and then dentistry school. But I hadn't gone through middle school. Even if I had, my parents couldn't afford the expense of dentistry school. I'd have to accept the fact that I could never be a dentist. I could never enter any profession. The next best thing, we finally decided, was for me to learn a trade—to become a dental technician.

Vater and I started making the rounds of dental labs. "No," the first owner said, "you can't miss work on Saturday." The second said "No." One after another said "No."

Finally, on the list of fourteen dental labs in the city of Breslau, there was only one more. The master dental technician who owned the lab rubbed his chin as he thought. "We work four hours on Saturday mornings." He looked out the window. "Hm-m-m. If you would work an hour extra each evening."

He was more thinking out loud than making any offers.

"And if you would clean the lab each Monday morning. *Ja.*" He looked me in the eye. "*Ja.* That would work. An hour longer each evening, and be here to start cleaning at six thirty on Monday mornings. Is it a deal?"

At fourteen, I signed a contract to be apprenticed for four years. I would finish eighth grade and then have three weeks off before my apprenticeship started.

In the meantime, Vater came home one day with a brand-new bicycle.

"It's for your birthday," Mutti said.

"You'll need dependable transportation to get the three miles across town for your work," Vater said.

"*Danka! Danka!*" I said, eyeing the light blue bicycle. "Thank you! Thank you!"

It was the most beautiful bicycle I'd ever seen. And brand new. It had wider tires than many bicycles—we called them half-balloon tires. On the cobblestone streets made of two-inch squares of granite, the tires sang. The faster I rode, the higher the tone. I loved hearing its music. After each ride, I carried my sturdy—and heavy—bicycle up the steps to our second-floor apartment and placed it on the balcony. There, I often dusted it, polished it, and oiled it.

As the end of school approached, an interesting thought crossed my mind. I looked at a map at school and started getting excited. *But Vater wouldn't let me do it,* I thought. *Maybe not,* I reasoned, *but he listened to me when I said I didn't want to be a gardener. What can it hurt to ask?*

At supper a few days later, Vater seemed to be in a pleasant mood. "I have an idea," I said. "The three weeks after I get out of school are the only vacation I'll have for the next four years. I'd like to take a trip—to ride my bicycle to visit our relatives in Saxony."

One of Vater's eyebrows twitched upward.

Mutti stopped chewing and looked up.

"I'm almost fifteen," I added.

"Ja, ja," Mutti said, "but—"

"He's taking a man's job," Vater said. He eyed me till I felt again like a little boy about to get into trouble. Finally, he looked back to Mutti. "And he's six feet tall. Why don't we let him?"

I took off on my bicycle the day after school was out. As soon as I was in the country, I breathed deeply of the clean air; marveled at the fields of waving grain just beginning to head; waved to farmers as they hoed rows of sugar beets and potatoes near the road; listened to the music of the tires change with the different kinds of roads—my favorites were the songs of the tires on roads built of granite squares or of asphalt.

By evening, I'd ridden 130 miles. At a youth hostel, I got an inexpensive meal and a place to sleep. A class of schoolgirls also stayed there overnight.

The next morning, I was up early. In the washroom I noticed a row of cups, each holding a toothbrush and container of toothpaste. I washed my face and brushed my teeth.

I grinned while I dumped water into a tub. When the water was several inches deep, I dumped all the cups, toothbrushes, and toothpaste into the water. Then I hit the road, laughing about all the commotion there would be when the girls got up.

The second day, I headed into the mountains . . . and into a head wind. This vacation was hard work. I rode 110 miles that day and was bushed. The next day I arrived in the state of Saxony. Over several days, I visited uncles, aunts, and cousins.

Money was even tighter in the state of Saxony than in the state of

Silesia where we lived, but my relatives welcomed me into their homes. Fried potatoes and eggs were staples there too. And, occasionally, *Kuchen*—a scrumptious, fruity cake.

I stayed two days with Grandfather Grellmann. He was as tall as I and had been muscular in earlier years. Grandmother had died, and Grandfather was lonely. He told me story after story from his life.

The second night when I hung my clothes in the wardrobe in the room where I slept, I noticed a metal box sitting at the back of the wardrobe, nearly hidden by a long wool coat. The box was about fourteen inches long, eight inches wide, and six inches deep. Curious, I opened it. My eyes got big. The box was filled with silver coins. I picked up a five-mark coin and looked at it. Almost before I knew what I was doing, I slipped the coin into my pocket, slid the lid back on the box, and closed the wardrobe.

The next morning when I was ready to head out the door, Grandfather said, "I am so glad you came to visit your old grandfather." He reached out to shake hands. Suddenly he pulled back. "Just a minute."

Grandfather turned and walked into the room where I had slept. I watched through the door as he opened the wardrobe. He slid the lid off the box of coins.

My heart raced. My throat went dry. My stomach churned.

A moment later he was back. "A gift to you, Grandson." He held out a silver five-mark coin.

My heart pounded. *What should I do?*

I reached out, and I tried to hold my voice steady. "Thank you, Grandfather."

As I rounded a bend on my bicycle, I looked back. Grandfather waved. I did too.

Shame filled me. It had been a good visit until I stole the coin.

For miles it seemed my bicycle tires had lost their song. Instead they chanted, "Thief . . . thief . . . thief."

*   *   *

After my vacation, life took on a new routine. On Mondays I got up at 5:00 A.M. After breakfast, I rode three miles to the center of town to a large red-brick building that housed several businesses. I carried my bicycle down the stairs to a storage room in the basement and climbed the stairs to the dental laboratory on the second floor. There I cleaned the laboratory counters and swept and mopped the floor before 8:00 A.M.

At first the technician work was more scary than interesting. From dentists, the other apprentice and I received the broken parts of impressions. We had to piece them together, then mix plaster to the right consistency to flow into, and fill, all the cavities of the impression . . . without causing bubbles. If we stirred the plaster too much, it would harden too fast. If we stirred it too little or added too much water, it would take longer to set and not be hard enough. When it was set, we carefully broke the impression off the model. If the teeth broke off also, we were in trouble.

Besides dentures, there were crowns, bridges, and single teeth to make. My fellow apprentice and I were always pushed for time—the six technicians had to wait for the models we made in order to begin their work. Gradually, step by step, we learned one process after another.

After I missed work the first Saturday, one of the technicians asked me why.

"I go to church on Saturday," I replied.

Another technician laughed. He looked up from his Bunsen burner. "Church?" he spluttered. "Church is bad enough. But why on Saturday?"

I tried to explain, but the razzing got worse. "Why don't you become a preacher?" one jeered.

"No sense in preaching," the first countered. "Politics is the important thing now."

A third joined in. "*Ja.* Religion's disappearing. German life is about politics now!"

I heard an instrument drop. "Hey, Grellmann," the second technician called, "I dropped my knife. Come pick it up for me."

I walked over, leaned down, grasped the handle of the knife, and started to pick it up. Suddenly, my fingers burned. I flung the instrument across the floor.

The three technicians who'd been razzing me burst into raucous laughter. I realized there was no reason for the handle to be hot. The technician had heated it in the flame of his Bunsen burner specifically to play a trick on me.

Week by week, the jeering got worse. The pranks got worse. It only heightened my discontent. I tried not to think about being shut out of what I really wanted to do, but sometimes the disappointment flooded over me in waves. I loved my ride home from work on Friday. I hated Monday mornings.

"I'm NOT going back!" I exploded one Monday evening when I arrived home.

That evening, and several others, Mutti encouraged me. Vater reminded me that I'd signed a contract, that a man was as good as his word. He said that the total impossibility of keeping a promise—as in death—was the only reason for breaking it.

Tuesday morning, I carried my bicycle down the stairs and pedaled toward the dental lab. I was stuck for four years—four l-o-n-g years.

At least the technicians couldn't fault the quality of my work. My grandfather's and father's skills with their hands seemed to have passed on to me. I worked hard to do a good job and to increase my speed.

As part of my apprenticeship, I attended weekly classes at a trade school. We studied general anatomy, physics, chemistry, metallurgy, and other subjects. "I have a suggestion for those of you who are dental technician apprentice students," our main teacher said one day. "You don't have to do it for a school assignment. It's something that will be just for your own benefit. But if you'll do it, it will help you excel."

I was all ears. If I was going to work as a dental technician for the rest of my life, I might as well be the best one I could be.

"Carve a set of teeth out of plaster of Paris," the teacher said.

I made an oblong block of plaster of Paris about five inches long. When it had hardened, I started carving a front tooth. The carving was tedious. Blisters formed on my hands as I carved one oversized tooth after another. But the extra project helped me work faster—after carefully examining and painstakingly carving each tooth, I easily recognized the shape of each and knew immediately where it belonged in the mouth.

During my second year, the same teacher encouraged me to participate in the annual *Reichsberufswettkampf*—National Trades and Occupations Competition. Young people from all the trades competed for recognition and scholarships.

"You have good skills," my teacher assured me. "And you have a good head."

I glanced around.

"Yes, I'm talking to you, Georg," the teacher said with a smile.

I flushed with embarrassment.

Should I try? I wondered that afternoon. *My teacher thinks I'm capable,* I thought. Then my heart beat faster. A knot started to grow in my stomach. *But Vater has known me longer . . . and he thinks I'm too stupid to learn.*

Should I Try?
1938

My teacher's and my father's opinions of my potential sparred in my mind. Who was right?

I could usually forget the mental boxing match over the weekends. One of the things I enjoyed in Breslau was the church youth group. About thirty young people gathered at the church on Friday evenings. We shared devotions. We rehearsed as a choir for worship services and for holiday programs such as Christmas and *Toten Sonntag*, a patriotic holiday honoring Germany's fallen. One group practiced with mandolins and guitars—I played my mother's mandolin. We planned outings—ice-skating, skiing, and in summer, hikes or picnics.

While other young men were getting interested in girls, my friend Herbert and I did interesting and important things—like, one Sunday morning, catching a mouse and placing it in a paper bag. We rolled the top closed, set the bag on the shelf in a telephone booth, and casually wandered to the street corner, where we could watch incognito.

Shortly, a young woman purposefully headed toward the phone booth. Before she made a call, she noticed the bag, looked around as if to see if anyone was returning for the treasure they'd accidentally left, and then, spotting no one, she reached for the bag.

The woman carefully unrolled the top and tipped her head down to inspect her find. She shrieked, dropped the bag, and bolted from the booth, down the street, and around a corner.

We nearly broke our sides with laughter. "Poor mouse," I said after I caught my breath. "He's going to get a punctured ear drum if we leave him there."

We retrieved the innocent creature. "Now what do we do with him?" Herbert wondered aloud.

As we walked along, bag in hand, an idea came to me. "The Schallers," I said. "We could take them a gift."

Herbert got a glint in his eye.

Pastor Schaller was our church's youth pastor. He and his wife lived on the top floor of a new apartment house a couple blocks away. We climbed the stairs and rang the doorbell.

No one answered. We rang the bell again. Not a sound from inside.

"Too bad," I said. "A bag full of fun and no one to enjoy it."

Herbert grinned. "Just a minute. Have a knife?"

"Yeah."

"Unscrew the brass plate with the doorbell."

It didn't take me long to get my jackknife out of my pocket and start loosening screws. When the cover came off, we encouraged Miss Mouse through the hole.

As I centered the cover over the hole to screw it back into place, I heard steps coming up the stairs. I glanced at Herbert, and his eyes got big.

"Let's go!"

I stuffed the hardware into my pocket as we headed down. It seemed as though my heart was beating louder than our footfalls on the steps. I heard a door slam on the floor below and then no more footsteps. We met no one on the steps. As we wandered down the street, I suggested, "We can give Pastor Schaller his doorbell this evening at the picnic."

"Perfect," Herbert agreed.

That evening Herbert and I arrived at the park together. Pastor and Frau Schaller were already surrounded by several of the youth group.

Frau Schaller was saying, "We don't know if someone tried to break in or what."

"I called the police," Pastor Schaller said, "as soon as we discovered the doorbell missing."

Uh-oh! I thought. I glanced at Herbert. His eyes met mine with a *What-do-we-do-now?* look. The brass bell and plate hung heavy in my pocket.

The topic of conversation at the picnic was the criminals who had stolen the pastor's doorbell and the evils of crime and the need for justice. I watched for opportunities to break Herbert's and my silence. No comfortable moment showed up. Besides, my tongue felt glued to the top of my mouth. The brass bell and plate seemed heavier in my pocket on the way home.

The next morning, I went to work a few minutes early—with the brass in my pocket. Not wanting to be caught with the evidence, I melted the bell and its plate down to a clod and threw it in the garbage. I heaved a sigh of relief to be done with the doorbell and went to work cleaning the lab and then making an impression for a dental plate.

Working on teeth reminded me about the National Trades and Occupation Competition. I could enter the citywide competition that year. Should I bother to try? Why not? The worst that preparing could do was help me become better at my trade.

I studied my textbooks all the harder and started memorizing the Periodic Chart of Elements: "Element—gold; Latin name—*aurum*; abbreviation—Au; specific gravity—19.3; melting point—1064.18 degrees centigrade. Element: silver; Latin name: *argentum*; abbreviation—Ag; specific gravity—10.5; melting point—961.78 degrees centigrade." And so on through the table of a hundred or so elements.

Sometimes I wondered whether the extra work was worthwhile. *Somehow,* I reminded myself, *someday, it will help me some way in my trade.*

One morning at 6:30, when I took my bicycle downstairs to the storage room, the basement reeked of a strange smell. The odor filled the stairwells and lab too. Sweeping and scrubbing didn't diminish the smell.

The first technician to arrive wrinkled his nose. *"Pee-eouw!"* he exclaimed. "What have you done to the lab?"

"Just cleaned it," I said. "Like always. As for the stink, it smelled like this when I arrived. It smells even worse in the basement."

Another technician came in. "Smells like liquor in here. Has Preacher Boy been imbibing?"

"Maybe something happened in the wholesale liquor store downstairs," the first technician said. He squinted as though he was thinking. "Be right back." He turned on his heels and disappeared out the door.

The rest of the technicians showed up for work, each with their own comments about the smell.

The first technician was back in minutes. "Herr Neumeier's store is in shambles. Someone broke in and smashed bottles left and right. Glass everywhere. Liquor standing on the floor. What a mess!"

The ensuing discussion ranged from "Who would do that?" to "Is there any damage in our lab?"

"I didn't see any damage when I was cleaning," I offered.

"Let's double check," the owner said. "Everyone check your own work area." As we headed to do so, he added, "And check to see if anything is missing. I'll check the supplies."

We inspected the place—nothing damaged, nothing missing.

"You know," one technician said thoughtfully, "on my way to work this morning, I saw a lot of broken glass on the sidewalks in one area. One display window after another was broken. I wonder why."

Vacation
1938

The next day, newspapers were full of stories about smashed windows all over Germany. The one thing they had in common was that the broken windows were all in businesses or homes owned by Jews. "Popular Demonstration Hits Jewish Businesses!" the headlines read. Some newspapers referred to that night as *Kristallnacht*—the night of broken glass.

At work, broken glass was the topic of discussion again.

"I don't know anyone who was involved in the destruction," one technician said.

"Me either," most agreed.

"I don't know who did it or why," one technician retorted, "but whoever it was ought to have to clean up the mess themselves and pay every mark it takes to repair the damage!"

"Maybe it wasn't really a popular demonstration," one said.

"I heard the SAs did all the damage," another added.

"Hm-m-m. Hitler's elite forces?" one questioned.

"No!" a third one countered. "All the SAs together *couldn't* have done that much damage!"

"Besides," the first technician added, "the government has worked for years to *build* the economy. Why would they damage businesses? That wouldn't make sense."

"None of it makes any sense to me," the owner concluded. "But one thing I do know—there are dentists waiting on the projects we have to do. We'd better get to work."

On the way to my work area, *das Vorurteil* crossed my mind. Prejudice. A lot of meanness must be hiding in someone's heart to have prejudice enough to destroy millions of marks' worth of assets belonging to one nationality of people.

*   *   *

I worked hard as my apprenticeship continued, and I studied hard. My skills improved. My employer gave me more advanced projects—crowns and bridges. My pocket money increased too. The first year I had received ten marks per month. I gave tithe and offering to the church and six marks to Mutti to help with food. I saved as much as possible of the rest because I needed a good warm coat. The second year I received fifteen marks a month. Finally, the third year, my pocket money was up to twenty marks.

After I saved for three years, Uncle Walter, who was a tailor, came to Breslau to sing in the annual German *Saengerfest*. Choirs came from all over Germany. Several thousand singers and a large orchestra assembled in Century Hall. The choirs sang old classics. They sang new patriotic songs. Applause exploded. "*Heil,* Hitler!" many shouted.

While Uncle Walter was at our house, I asked him how much he'd charge to make me a warm winter coat.

"Depends on how much material it will take," he said. "Come here, let me measure you."

He took more measurements than I knew I had and then did a few calculations. "The cloth will cost eighty marks," he said.

I waited. He just looked at me as though he was expecting a response. "How much to make it?" I asked.

"Nothing, Georg!"

"But—"

He waved me to silence. "I'll only accept enough for the cost for the material," he said. "I'd consider it a pleasure to make you a coat."

"Be back in a minute," I said. I pulled out the tin box in the back of my clothing drawer. *What a blessing he's not charging for labor,* I thought. I carried all of my savings except seven marks to Uncle Walter. "Here it is," I said. "Make me a coat."

Finally, after three years, I kept warm on my way to work through the cold months!

Through the winter I worked and studied hard. Then came the spring of 1939 and the National Trades and Occupations competition.

My work paid off in the first competition. During the written tests, I easily recalled the answers. The practical tests went fairly well too.

On awards day, I was recognized as best dental technician appren-

tice in my city and received a bronze medal—the top medal for each citywide competition.

That felt good! I *was* good at something.

Then I studied all the harder—winning the city competition qualified me to compete at the state level.

Since Breslau was the capital of Silesia, I didn't need to travel for the state compe-

*Bronze medal—*Kreissieger *(krei = town)*

tition. The tests at the state level were a lot harder than the city test—more and harder questions in one's technical area, in history, and in general knowledge. I wasn't nearly as confident about how I'd done.

At the awards ceremony, however, I was pronounced *Gausieger*—winner in the state—and awarded the highest medal, silver.

*Silver medal—*Gausieger *(gau = state)*

I wore my medal home. "Congratulations, Son!" Mutti enthused. She got excited about my success. Vater said nothing.

Winning the state medal qualified me to compete at the national level. But would it be worth the trouble? *The tests will be even harder,* I reasoned. *And the competition at nationals will be even stiffer.*

The idea of winning the national competition was more than I could even dream. But what did I have to lose? I'd get to travel by train at government expense, to explore an area I had never seen. Besides, I'd get two and a half weeks off work.

Ah-h-h. Time off work. Two and a half weeks away from chemicals and acids, from the process of polishing that filled the air with polluting particles and made tuberculosis a hazard of the trade.

I doubted I had even half a chance to win, but that didn't matter. I would take my tests, and I would have a grand vacation traveling, enjoying fresh air, exploring a new town, and relishing my freedom.

Knowing a break was coming up, I worked with new enthusiasm.

The badge confirming that I was a participant in *Reichsberufswettkampf* was my train ticket to Cologne. Representatives from every trade in every German state converged for the National Trades and Occupations Competition. Since I knew I couldn't possibly win, I told myself, *Time off work! Enjoy!*

The first Monday we started hour after grueling hour of written tests in varied subjects—language, mathematics, history, and others. Of course, they asked Hitler's birthday. That was easy for me to remember—mine was the same day, April 20.

For several more days, everyone took tests in their own discipline. "Do your best," one of our leaders reminded us. "Remember, the winner gets a full, four-year oral surgeon scholarship at the University of Koenigsberg."

That was well and good. And I would do my best—just to see what I could do. But I knew winning the scholarship wasn't even a possibility. I was having fun seeing the sights of Cologne in the evenings, and I would be happy with that.

For several days, the participants did practical, hands-on work in their own trade. I was glad I had worked hard and done my best in my apprenticeship.

Last, we competed in sports. Even though I completed the races within the required time, I came in dead last in the one hundred-meter dash *and* in the three thousand-meter race. If I had had even the slightest chance of winning. Surely my poor showing in sports definitely put an end to that.

No problem, I reminded myself. *The chances of my winning were next to nil anyway—the competition is fierce. Every person here is the best in their trade from their state. Just getting to come is an honor. I'm here just to enjoy the experience, and*—I smiled to myself at the thought—*I'm missing work.*

On Sunday afternoon several thousand participants met in a huge hall—a sea of the brown shirts of the Hitler Youth. An orchestra played. A speech followed. Then the winners were announced. One winner after another marched to the platform to the music of thunderous applause. It went on . . . and on . . . for some time.

I was joking with the young man beside me when it seemed I heard the announcer's voice say, "Georg Grellmann." My heart nearly stopped. I blinked. *Couldn't have been,* I thought. *But it sure sounded like it.* I looked around in my section. No one else was getting up. Several motioned toward me. "Get up! *Ja!* It is you!"

My heart pounded as I stood. The applause was deafening. I floated rather than walked toward the front of the auditorium.

"Congratulations, Herr Grellmann!" the announcer said when I stepped onto the platform.

Applause continued as I stepped forward to a government official. He pinned the gold medal over my heart and handed me a winner's certificate. My head felt as though it was spinning. I shook hands with that official and several others.

I stood there as if in shock. My mind whirled: . . . *gold medal . . . national winner . . . scholarship . . . university . . . oral surgeon . . . I can go to the university! . . . I can be a dentist!*

Gold medal—Reichssieger *(*reich = nation*)*

My heart pounded in my throat, and my head felt as though it might explode. *I'm going to the university!* I wanted to shout. I floated back to my seat.

Can this be real? I took a deep breath and looked at the certificate—those near me strained to see it too. The front was gold embossed with the German eagle. I unfolded the left side, then the right. The certificate was about fourteen inches wide and nine inches high. On the left was Hitler's picture with his signature. On the right, all the particulars in Gothic letters and more official signatures.

Pride, joy, and excitement welled up inside me. *Finally,* I thought. *Finally . . . an impossible dream is reality! I'm going to do what I want to do! I am going to be an oral surgeon!*

My heart was pounding in my chest. *I have talent!* I told myself. *I am capable!*

At the end of the awards ceremony, another official made an announcement: "All of you who have won awards today, meet here tomorrow morning at eight o'clock with your bags. We will take the train to Berlin. Our Fuehrer, Adolf Hitler, wants to meet and congratulate each of you.

"We have honored national champion men and women today," the official continued. "But the reason all of you are here is that you, too, are highly skilled. Your dedication to excellence is a part of what makes Germany great!"

The orchestra hit a chord and started to play the national anthem, *"Deutschland, Deutschland."* A whoosh went through the auditorium as thousands of young men and women jumped to their feet. Their voices rang out, and the huge hall reverberated with the song.

> Unity and right and freedom for the German fatherland;
> Let us all pursue this purpose brotherly with heart and hand.
> Unity and right and freedom are the pledge of happiness.
> Flourish in this blessing's glory, flourish, German fatherland.

When we were free to go, a crowd of my dental technician competitors congratulated me. The judges in our section stayed by also. "Congratulations!" one said. "Are you aware that you are the first ever dental technician participant to win a gold medal?"

My mouth must have dropped open.

"No one else has ever reached the minimum score—one hundred and fourteen out of one hundred and twenty possible points. When we added points from the different disciplines, yours totaled one hundred and fourteen."

"Yeah, Grellmann!" other participants cheered, several slapping me on the shoulder. "You put us on the map!"

"You have excelled in your trade," one of the judges said as he pumped my hand. "May you excel as an oral surgeon!"

After supper at my hosts' home, I excused myself and walked the streets of Cologne, trying to use the energy that pounded through my arteries. I was almost afraid I would wake up and find the whole day had been a dream. Yet, I was awake. I stopped under a lamp and tipped up the gold medal on my lapel. It felt like the bronze and silver medals. But this was different—*"Reichssieger,"* winner for the nation. This medal meant my dreams were no longer impossible.

The next morning I thanked my host family and left for the hall in plenty of time. "There's been a change," an official announced. "Our Fuehrer has been called away from Berlin to meet with England's Prime Minister Chamberlain about a crisis of German people in Czechoslovakia. Hitler asked me to tell you that he knows he must attend this meeting for the benefit of all German people, but he regrets missing the opportunity to meet each of you. He said to remind you that the skills of people like you are what make Germany great.

"Since we will not be able to see our Fuehrer," the announcer continued, "you are now free to go back to your own homes. But Hitler did insist I tell you one more thing. He said to give you his personal congratulations! He is very proud of you!"

I wore the gold medal on the train. Since I couldn't go to Berlin, I decided to stop in Hamburg to visit Aunt Liesel and Uncle Fritz. I hadn't seen them since I was a young child, but I enjoyed Aunt Liesel's friendly letters to Mutti and all of us. I found the apartment that matched their address and rang the doorbell.

After a minute, Uncle Fritz opened the door.

"Georg Grellmann . . ." I said.

His expression darkened. The door slammed in my face.

Changes
1939

I stood outside the door in shock. Granted, it had been years since Uncle Fritz had seen me, but I had said my name. *What do I do now?* I wondered.

After a moment the door opened a crack. Glowering, Uncle Fritz asked, "What name did you say?"

"Georg Grellmann," I answered.

"Gertrud's son?"

"Yes."

He swung the door wide and looked me over from head to foot. Still scowling, he motioned me in. "Come in, Georg." He closed the door behind me. "Liesel," he called, "we have company."

Aunt Liesel came, drying her hands on her apron.

"It's Georg," Uncle Fritz said. "Your sister Gertrud's son."

"Why, Georg," Aunt Liesel said, and a smile lighted up her face. Her eyes danced. "So good to have you come! How are you? How is your mama? Do come in." Her voice sounded like happy music. She took my elbow and drew me to the couch. "Sit down. Sit down. Tell me about yourself and your family."

Uncle Fritz eyed me with suspicion as Aunt Liesel and I shared family news. Finally, Uncle Fritz could stand it no longer. "Why," he broke in, "are you wearing the Hitler Youth uniform?"

"I'm headed home from the National Trades and Occupations Competition in Cologne," I said. "Everyone had to wear the uniform."

"Are you a member of the Hitler Youth?"

"I joined," I admitted. "But all the marching and singing bores me. I haven't gone for several months."

"Do they bother you about not going?"

"Never have," I answered, "though Vater worries that my not attending may cause me trouble someday."

"Well, I wouldn't be surprised," Uncle Fritz snapped. "But you may be in more trouble if you go than if you don't."

"What do you mean?" I asked.

"I tell you," Uncle Fritz said, shaking his head. "I tell you, the Nazi party is trouble. The reason I shut the door on you was that you were wearing their uniform. If you hadn't said your name, you could have stood there till you rotted."

"I wore the uniform because it was required for the competition," I said. "But given the choice of the Communist Party and the Nazi party, I prefer the Nazis. Look what they're doing to improve the economy. More and more people are working. Food is more available since they took power."

"That's true," Uncle Fritz said. "But I still don't like them!"

No matter what I said, there was no convincing Uncle Fritz that the Nazi party was in any way desirable. But, finally, he took his eyes off my uniform long enough to notice the gold medal pinned to it.

Aunt Liesel gushed with pride.

"Congratulations," Uncle Fritz said. "I'm proud of you." The hint of a smile flashed, and then his expression darkened again. "I hope your dreams work out."

I couldn't understand the doubt in his voice.

We visited for a couple of hours before I headed back to the train station and took the train toward home.

Changes

The next afternoon when I arrived at our apartment house, Vater was coming down the stairs. We met on a landing. He embraced me and kissed me.

I stood there, mouth agape.

Vater headed back up the steps. Not hearing steps behind him, he turned, motioning for me to join him. "Come, come," he urged.

Neighbors from across the hall followed us into our apartment. Father smiled, proudly motioning my way. "He's a Grellmann," he bragged.

It was the first time I'd detected pride in Vater's voice when he spoke of me.

* * *

The days of freedom had been wonderful. But the next morning, I dusted off my bicycle and headed downtown to work.

"Congratulations," my master said. "You have done well. I am canceling the last six months of your apprenticeship. I will sign the papers showing you have finished your apprentice work and are a journeyman dental technician. Would you consider continuing working for me?"

My heart beat a little faster. *"J-j-ja,"* I stammered, my mind running on ahead of my mouth. The last six months of my apprenticeship, I was scheduled to receive thirty marks a month. The average dental technician earned about one hundred and fifty marks, unless they did crowns, bridges, and ceramic work—which I did.

My master went on, "I'll pay you two hundred and fifty marks a month."

It didn't take me long to agree to stay for a while.

Life became a little more relaxed for me. I still worked hard and learned, but I wasn't studying every spare minute. I took time to enjoy the beautiful city I lived in. In earlier times, Breslau had been a fortified city. A deep, wide moat still surrounded the old inner city, graced by picturesque bridges and delightful parks.

Breslau was proud of its museums, art galleries, orchestra, opera, theater, and cathedrals. I attended lectures at the university—one was by a professor who demonstrated the electronic microscope he had invented. It magnified ten thousand to thirty thousand times. I was impressed! I enjoyed the annual trade fair at Century Hall. I saw an early television there. The pictures were black and white and about the quality of pictures in newspapers. Century Hall also hosted many classical concerts—I attended at every opportunity I had. Each year my heart especially thrilled at the peace and majesty of Handel's *Messiah*.

More relaxation also meant I could spend more time with my friend Herbert and with the rest of the church youth group. Sometimes it was after dark when the Friday evening meetings let out. Herbert and I did our heroic duty and walked some of the girls home. Over the weeks, I found that Hanne (Hon´ na) and I seemed to gravitate toward each other on those trips.

One evening Hanne was talking to Frau Schaller. "Go ahead," I told Herbert. "You take the other girls home. I'll wait and walk Hanne home."

Herbert raised his eyebrows and then grinned and winked.

I started living for the Friday-night walk with Hanne. One night my heart was pounding in my throat as we neared her home. "May I kiss you?" I asked.

Hanne's smile and her kiss set my heart on fire.

* * *

In September of 1939, Vater got a draft notice. He was forty-three. That month, Germany and Russia attacked Poland. By September 28, Poland had surrendered. Referring to the defeat, Hitler quoted Scripture: *"Mit Mann und Ross und Wagen hat sie der Herr geschlagen!* [The Lord slew them with their men, horses, and wagons!]"

Vater was in the army on bicycle patrol for a month and then back home. He never saw military action. "The worst thing I saw," he told us, "was one soldier chasing a woman into a house. 'No! No!' she screamed. I tore in after them. 'Let loose of her!' I ordered. He did. 'Get out of this house!' He did. I followed him out and made sure he kept going."

German troops were welcomed in Austria, I thought. *And we conquered Poland in no time. German people will be reunited quickly and near painlessly for us Germans. And I'll go to gymnasium and then head for the University of Koenigsberg.* I smiled at the thought of getting on with my dream.

That winter, Hitler gave orders to build fortifications along the border with France, the Siegfried Line. I received my own personal letter from the German government instructing me to report at Kohlhoehe, near Brieg, for *Reichsarbeitsdienst*—a youth work camp started by Hitler to teach young men and women discipline, hard work, and the equality of people from all classes of society.

In peaceful times, the young men in the camps marched and worked to build up the country. They drained marshes, planted trees, and helped with harvesting. Since war had started before I was inducted, rather than the previous totally peaceful operations, our discipline included pre-military training. We marched with shovels on our shoulders, where guns would be later. We dug trenches and buried cables to bunkers where bombs were stored.

A young man used to studying or working at a desk all day got the same assignment as one whose muscles rippled because he had come from working on a farm or in the coal mines. A common assignment was to dig a trench two feet wide and five feet deep. The length for each day's assignment was determined according to the condition of the soil—big rocks, small stones, clay, or sand. When one's section of trench for that day met inspection, he could quit. Weekend leave was denied those who didn't complete their daily assignments.

The ground was so rocky we used picks as much as shovels. Sweat burned my eyes as I dug. My muscles ached—my previous work had kept me sitting in a laboratory. But I had learned perseverance. As my muscles and stamina grew, my workdays shortened.

As if a day digging wasn't enough, we also trained in various sports—gymnastics, running, boxing. At first, after three rounds of boxing, I felt like I might collapse. After the first day of digging and boxing, I was so exhausted I figured I'd sleep through any amount of foolishness or snoring in the crowded barracks. True to my suspicions, I dropped right off to sleep.

Georg in work camp. Besides eating utensils and blanket, his pack is likely filled with bricks.

Suddenly, the lights blazed on. The *Sturmfuehrer*—similar to a corporal in a military setting—stood inside the door. "Run!" he roared. "Around the barracks! No time for boots!"

Feet hit the floor running. The clock said midnight.

When we got back, he ordered, "Empty your mattress bags here! Report in front of the barracks with your empty bag for inspection! Quick!"

I grabbed my mattress-shaped bag filled with straw and dumped the contents on the floor as every other half-asleep draftee did. We ran outside and lined up, barefoot and pajama-clad, each holding an empty mattress bag.

When we each were in position, he barked, "Fill your bags. Room inspection in fifteen minutes."

We rushed inside and scooped straw into our bags, bounced the bags on the floor so there was more room, and scooped more straw. We made our beds and dusted our dressers the best we could with clouds of dust still billowing about the room.

The adrenaline from anger helped us hurry. The thirty in our room reassembled our bunks and were picking up a few stray straws when the *Sturmfuehrer* strode in. "By your bed!"

Each young man moved to the head of his bed.

"Attention!"

We froze at attention.

The *Sturmfuehrer* found a piece of straw under one bed. "Run!" he ordered. "To the bunkers and back! On the double!"

I wanted to crawl back into bed and believe the whole thing was a nightmare. I ran . . . along with everyone else.

On the weekend, I walked the two and a half miles from Kohl-hoehe to Brieg and rode the train twenty-five miles home to Breslau. Hanne's smile had never looked so sweet. Mutti's cooking had never tasted so good. Undisturbed sleep had never felt so wonderful.

On Sunday evening, I took the train back to Brieg. About thirty others from the work camp rode the same train. It was scheduled to arrive at 9:10 P.M. That would give us time to walk back to camp by our 10:00 P.M. curfew.

Our muscles grew through the weeks of work and sports. Our obe-dience got quicker. Unfortunately, midnight inspections didn't cease. We rushed, but even if we got our ransacked beds reassembled, the corporal, at the very least, found a bit of dust on the top of someone's makeshift closet.

"Run!" he ordered each time.

The treatment was unreasonable. I wanted to object. But others had tried that, and it only brought worse trouble. The major discipline of the work camp was learning to obey orders . . . immediately . . . without question . . . no matter what the orders.

Because Germany was at war, our group's service was extended from six months to nine. There was nothing we could do except stay, continue to work hard, and try to stay out of trouble.

Some weekends I visited family friends in Brieg. One Friday when I arrived, Frau Schaeffer was crying and Herr Schaeffer seemed sub-dued. Before long, the story spilled out.

"Herr and Frau Koehler have been our neighbors for several years," Herr Schaeffer said.

"Nice people," Frau Schaeffer added. "They and their four bright-eyed children."

"Herr Koehler owned a grocery store," Herr Schaeffer continued. "They had a nice house and seemed to be doing very well . . . until this week." Herr Schaeffer sighed and then went on. "Monday he got a draft notice. He went to the induction center to tell them he'd be glad to serve the country some other way but he could not serve as a soldier."

Frau Schaeffer sniffled.

Her husband swallowed hard. "They took him out and shot him."

"Didn't he know that's what they do?" I asked.

"Yes," Herr Schaeffer answered. "He knew."

I shook my head, hardly believing what I'd heard. "Why would he refuse to go into the army when he knew he would be shot?" I asked.

"He believed," Herr Schaeffer said with conviction. He took a deep breath. "He was a Jehovah's Witness, and he believed . . . that he should do ill to no man."

Sunday evening my footfalls ground into the gravel as I walked back to camp. I couldn't get the image out of my mind of a young widow dressed in black with four sad-eyed children following her. The story haunted me. *Why would a man desert his wife and children?* I wondered. *Why would he refuse to be inducted into the army when he knew he'd be shot? Didn't he benefit from the government in peacetime? Shouldn't he support the country in time of war too?*

Boot Camp
1941

I turned nineteen while in youth work camp. When I was released, I knew it wouldn't be long until I was drafted into the army. My old boss was delighted to put me back to work, even temporarily. Working for him didn't seem nearly as distasteful as it had early in my training. Besides, I had time to treasure family and friends—especially Hanne.

Sometimes I pondered war. The Jehovah's Witness father who chose to be shot rather than go to war needled me. What was a Christian's responsibility to his country?

One weekend a guest speaker spoke at church. He began, "Our beloved country is at war. How should we relate to our government during wartime? Should our young men go off to fight?"

He had my attention.

The minister spoke of duty to God and duty to country. He mentioned the many wars in the early days of Israel. He reminded us that Saul was moved to war against the Ammonites when the Spirit of God came upon him, as described in 1 Samuel 11. Jesus Himself said, "Render to Caesar the things that are Caesar's, and to God the things that are God's" (Mark 12:17). Paul said, "Let every soul be subject unto the higher powers [government]. For there is no power but of God: the powers that be are ordained of God" (Romans 13:1). He continued to cite verses, including, "Whosoever therefore resisteth the power, resisteth the ordinance of God: and they that resist shall receive to themselves damnation" (Romans 13:2).

So, if God ordained the current government, shouldn't we support it?

One evening Vater said, "Georg, Mutti and I are concerned about you. Surely you've thought about what's coming." Silence hung between us.

"You mean the army?" I asked.

"Yes," he responded. "You've gone to church all your life. You've heard the Bible. You've heard the stories. What do you think about God? What do you think about baptism?"

I sensed my parents' concern for not just my spiritual life but my physical life, as well. I believed there was a God. I wanted to live right. And I believed baptism was the right thing to do. On Friday evening a couple weeks later, a pastor from a different church in the city baptized another young man, and Vater baptized me. I vowed I would be true to God.

Days later, a lump formed in my throat when a letter addressed to me arrived. I slid my finger under the flap and opened the single sheet: "You will report to the German army infantry October 12, 1940 at 0900 . . ."

October 12? Only two days away. The days went by in a whirl—quitting my job, savoring home cooking, treasuring last moments, bidding farewell. Hanne and I treasured each moment we could spend together. I savored the sense of our last hug, our last kiss. We promised to be true to each other.

Then came the tram trip to the train station. Mutti went with me. She put on a brave front, but fear filled her eyes.

Young men and their families crowded together in the broad cobblestone commons in front of the depot. Too soon, an army officer and his loudspeaker began spitting names. One by one, young men left their families and formed a tidy line in front of the officer. Then I heard, "Georg Grellmann."

I turned to look at Mutti one last time.

"I will pray for you," she whispered. "Every day."

*   *   *

I was just one of two hundred young men who disappeared into the depot, marched out the back, and climbed aboard a train. It chugged west across Germany's central highlands—up and down the hills, by newly harvested fields, past one village after another. Three days later we crossed the River Rhine, entering Alsace-Lorraine. Germany had lost it to France in the Treaty of Versailles at the end of World War I. Now, earlier in the year, Germany had won back the area.

The brick barracks on the outskirts of the town of Metz had been built by the French for their army. Privacy was unheard of—all the washrooms and toilets were open. Six or more men slept in a room. The beds were hard and the barracks and mess hall unheated.

"Primitive," one young man sneered.

Nobody disagreed.

Boot camp. Marching was the first order of business. Woe to the man whose heel slapped the cobblestones slightly out of sync.

Obeying orders was also first and last and every time in between.

As our training progressed, anything we'd missed about the word *obey* in work camp became resoundingly clear in boot camp.

How to maintain and handle a gun was drilled into us. "Treat it like your bride!" the officers barked. We had to throw ourselves into puddles and mud, but our "bride" had to stay clean and dry. We learned to protect our guns, whatever it took. Without a gun, we would be defenseless.

We learned to use gas masks, machine guns, hand grenades—every weapon we might be called upon to use.

We marched with gas masks impeding our breathing, with the backpacks filled with forty pounds of bricks.

"Run!" our instructor, Corporal Schmidt, commanded.

We did.

"Hit the ground!"

We did.

"Run!"

We ran.

"Sing!"

We sang a patriotic song.

"Louder!" Corporal Schmidt ordered.

We sang as best we could while running.

"Faster!"

Some collapsed.

We learned to dig foxholes—fast—to stay alive. We learned to keep our heels and head down flat to the ground to avoid catching bullets.

Some training situations just begged for a witty remark. Sometimes I succumbed and made a comment. Those nearby would laugh.

"Around the barracks!" Corporal Schmidt barked. "Ten times. On the double!"

We all ran.

Sometimes when we were in clean uniforms, the corporal marched us into mud. "Down!" he yelled.

We hit gooey soil, stomach down.

"Forward on your elbows—like a snake!"

He egged us on till we were filthy to our skin and then marched us back to our barracks, dismissed us, then barked, "Inspection in thirty minutes!"

Uniforms could be wet but had to be clean.

There wasn't enough time. That was the point. He could punish us if we were late or had missed a speck of dirt someplace on our uniform. "Hit the ground. Push-ups till I tell you to quit!"

Patriotic quotations of poets and philosophers decorated every wall in the barracks and mess hall. One by Nietzsche read, "The individual is nothing. The nation is everything."

How does God relate to that? I wondered.

I believed in God and the Bible. But at home, decisions had been made by Vater. I'd had little experience thinking things through for myself. *Is our purpose only realized in the context of living for a nation?* I wondered from time to time. *Who decides if war is necessary for the survival of the nation?*

We weren't given much time for thinking. If we weren't drilling, often we were pressing uniforms, shining boots, or running errands for various sergeant majors or corporals. If we did a particularly good job for them, they sometimes offered to do a favor for us. My request was for their leftover bread. Army rations were none too generous. As a lean, six-foot-two-inch nineteen-year-old getting more exercise than I'd ever imagined, I was always hungry. I relished whatever bread they shared, no matter how dry it was.

After an exhausting, demoralizing eight weeks, we were allowed to leave the base for the first time . . . in the company of our corporal at all times.

Corporal Schmidt and his fifteen draftees headed straight for a restaurant. Along with their meals, the others ordered beer or liquor. I ordered lemonade.

After several drinks, one soldier began flirting with waitresses. She winked and flashed him a smile. "Want another beer?"

"*Ja, ja.*"

"One for me too," another soldier added.

"And me."

"Me also."

"Another round?" another waitress questioned.

"*Ja, ja,*" the soldiers responded.

They each got their beers. I wished I could leave. But orders were orders—I had to stay with Corporal Schmidt. And he was every bit a part of the frivolity. I downed another lemonade.

The more beer consumed, the more the soldiers and the corporal vied for the attention of the waitresses. The comments got lewd. One soldier after another kissed a waitress, and the waitresses acted as though they enjoyed the attention of these strangers.

The behavior disgusted me.

Finally, about 11:00 P.M., the rest of the men stumbled back to the barracks. At last, I was free from the fetid odor and embarrassing behavior. I pictured Hanne with her sparkling gray-green eyes, her warm smile. *I didn't compromise my promise tonight,* I thought. *And I never will.*

The next day, Corporal Schmidt called me aside. "Last night, it was unfair of you not to drink liquor with your comrades."

I blinked, hardly believing what I had heard.

His stare remained firm.

"It was pretty obvious where the liquor led," I wanted to shout back. "I want no part of your lack of morals!" But I knew better than to say anything.

"You are part of a group, Grellmann," he admonished. "Don't set yourself apart."

Orders are orders. I kept my mouth shut, but I vowed I'd not do anything that would make me act as foolish as my comrades had the night before. I wouldn't do anything that would compromise my promise to Hanne or decrease my ability to make good decisions—decisions that soon might make the difference between life and death.

One morning a sergeant major showed up at inspection and asked, "Who knows how to ski?"

Skiing brought up pleasant images in my mind. I'd been taught to be honest, so I, along with several others, raised my hand.

We were allowed to leave the ranks, but only to go to the nearby Mosel Mountains. We each drilled with winter coat, rifle, gas mask, steel helmet, shovel, backpack—the entire front-line outfit. Day after day, we transported ammunition and other supplies, or a "wounded" man, up and down the overgrown hills. To make matters worse, we had to keep constant watch so we didn't fall into the battle scars of World War I—craters left from grenade explosions or brush-covered crevasses that had been sections of trenches. This skiing was not at all like times on the slopes with Hanne!

Back at camp, occasionally the soldiers with the best target shooting practice got a day off. My steady hand with both rifle and pistol worked to my advantage. Not only did I enjoy the days off, but also I went into town and bought grape jam or a thick chocolate paste to spread on the dry bread I received from various officers. Even so, by the end of boot camp, I had lost ten pounds.

After boot camp, we were moved to a German army base at Idar-Oberstein. Our company was assigned to the Alsace-Lorraine Double Cross Division. Then we headed for Russia.

We were no longer a dozen individuals each making his own decision. We were one unit—a family, of sorts. Our purpose was to defend our homeland, to protect our mothers and sweethearts. We had an enemy to fight. Following orders had become almost automatic.

Our train traveled east across Germany. No colorful flowers graced the towns. The autumn foliage had fallen, leaving bare limbs and dead fields.

Our train crossed into Poland in the morning. After breakfast I threw a banana peel out the window. A skinny boy picked the peeling off the ground and stuffed it into his mouth. I stared in disbelief.

As he chewed, a small piece of peeling protruded. A bigger boy grabbed the corner of yellow and yanked, getting a square. He greedily shoved it into his own mouth.

My jaw dropped. How hungry they must be!

I watched out the window with a new sadness. All across the country, children with hollow eyes begged for food as our train passed. War had likely killed many of their parents or imprisoned their fathers in some faraway prisoner-of-war camp.

When we reached the Polish/Russian border at Przemysl, we changed onto Russian trains with wider gauge tracks. At that point we left the comfortable passenger trains and piled onto a freight train. A small coal-burning iron stove stood in one corner of our boxcar. Between it and our body heat, we kept nearly warm enough. Straw on the floor cushioned our sitting or lying down.

The train stopped often—usually to let supply trains pass, sometimes to let us relieve ourselves and for us to receive food. Whenever the boxcar door was unlocked, I got out to stretch my legs and snag a few breaths of fresh air.

In one village, walking along the train toward the station, I noticed a pit. I looked down. There lay the bodies of six nude men as they'd been tossed—their arms, legs, and heads splayed haphazardly, blood and bullet wounds clearly visible.

I felt sick to my stomach. I turned away, swallowing hard to keep my lunch down.

Inside the station, I heard the supposed story—these six partisans, guerrilla fighters, had blown up a train loaded with German soldiers behind our front line. As a warning, their bodies would be displayed for three days before they would be buried.

Were they really partisans? I wondered. *Or were they just in the wrong place at the wrong time?*

Our train lumbered on. Within a few hours, it stopped again. But this time was different.

The boxcar door was unlocked. The order rang out, "Fall in." As we assembled, our breath was visible in the crisp air. Artillery and machine-gun fire rang out in the distance.

It took several days for us to get organized. We slept in the homes of the village. Each soldier was assigned his weapon—rifle, machine gun, grenade thrower. We were given ammunition.

Then we marched, our steps muffled by the snow. The farther we went, the louder the gun reports.

Drilling was over. This was war.

Enemies
1942

A series of trenches zigzagged across the plains. The men in these front line trenches had shaggy beards, hair hanging below their helmets, faces tanned from sun reflecting on snow. I expected our front line troops to be glad to see a division of freshly trained reinforcements to replace their dead and wounded. The soldiers didn't welcome us—just looked at us and then looked away.

There in the trench, the possibility of death—or, worse, of becoming a prisoner of war—suddenly became real. My heart pounded. My throat went dry. My breaths came shallow. I realized my mind wasn't as clear as it needed to be if I was to accomplish my patriotic duty *and* to have a chance of surviving long enough to hold Hanne again.

Suddenly, in my mind's eye, I was back at the train depot in Breslau. Mutti looked into my eyes—"I will pray for you," she whispered. "Every day."

On the front line, I sensed that fear would kill me, one way or another. I would have to depend on my family praying for me. I chose not to think about the possible calamities but instead to keep alert for the present instant.

From the moment we arrived, we were part of the war effort, pushing the Russian front line east. In one of the first battles in which we took a village, Russian soldiers' bodies lay scattered. I had an odd sense of sadness at the loss of life and yet relief that it was the enemy that was dead. Walking by one dead soldier, I noticed something he had carried. Curious, I leaned down and opened the case—it held a German-made camera. He had probably taken it from a dead German soldier in a previous battle. Anger welled up in me at men who killed my comrades and stole their belongings; anger at having to be here shooting and dodging bullets; anger at war; anger at death.

Occasionally one of our German soldiers was killed. Only a few days passed till one of my group fell. We had trained together, eaten together, gotten in trouble together, traveled to Russia together, and now fought together. On the battlefield, we held our position till nightfall, and then I and others in my group, under the cover of darkness, dug a shallow grave. We laid our fallen comrade in it, said the Lord's Prayer, and buried our friend.

The questions were harder to bury. We had done our best for him, but the picture of my friend and comrade lying dead on the Ukrainian plain was etched into my memory. I couldn't close my eyes without seeing him. Fear and grief threatened to paralyze me. But I dared not let it. I had to keep every sense engaged at all times.

If it was quiet during the long, cold days, some of us could catch a nap in the trench or dream of home and sweethearts. Sometimes I slipped Hanne's photo out from between the pages of the small Bible in my pocket and dreamed of better days. But always, through the longer, colder nights, every soldier had to be awake and on alert. At first we kept the Russian front line retreating. We moved forward and occupied the Russian troops' last trenches. Sometimes we dug our own foxholes and then, if we were in one spot for any length of time, dug between our foxholes to join them into trenches.

One tactic we used to speed Russian retreat was to focus on one point. We would break through with tanks, followed by swarms of infantry. We moved as far as we could as fast as we could, forcing the rest of their front line back.

We got used to the different weapons the Russians used on us. There was the *rat-a-tat-tat-tat* of machine-gun fire; the *cr-r-a-a-ck* of a T-34 tank shot, the whistle as the shell came closer.

The grenade throwers shot their grenades high till they descended like bombs, sometimes into a foxhole or trench. Even if you were in the open, by the time you heard them, it was too late. You didn't even have time to throw yourself to the ground.

We hated the eerie wail of the Stalin-organ. It combined several grenade throwers, and its grenades were calculated to land close together, carpeting the area and causing uniform devastation, similar to carpet bombing. Everything and everyone in the targeted area got hit.

During lulls in the fighting, there was some opportunity to talk with comrades. When we were east of Kharkov, gradually the veteran soldiers began to share their experiences with those of us who had survived our first few weeks on the battlefront. The previous autumn, still in summer uniforms, they'd been moving toward Moscow. Columns of tanks dashed ahead to encircle the city. When the tanks got within twenty miles of the city, winter hit—unusually sudden, unusually early, unusually severe. The wheels of vehicles and tracks of tanks froze overnight in the mud. The men were freezing. They had to leave the equipment and try to get back to their main positions.

Some days were so cold that metal contracted till guns wouldn't shoot. Engines wouldn't start. Only mines and hand grenades would work. Men's ears, noses, and feet froze. The ground was frozen too hard to dig trenches. War came to a standstill—soldiers on both sides were simply trying to keep warm enough to survive. When it warmed up, fighting resumed.

"The killing gets to me," one soldier admitted with a sigh. "All the Ivan." (We referred to the Russians as Ivan.) "Ivan attacked in wave after wave. Of course, we fought back—self-preservation. They just kept coming. We kept shooting. Bodies piled on top of bodies." My comrade shuddered. "To advance, you had to walk over them." He shook his head. "There's no heroism in that. It's carnage."

"Ja," another said. "Life seemed so cheap and futile."

Another added, "At first, fear grips you. But you can't change the situation. If you dare to think about it, you can't stand it." Silence hung in the chill air for a long time until he swallowed hard and went on: "But you come more or less to stoic acceptance—just do what you have to do to try to survive."

His words came back to me often. Just do what you have to do to try to survive.

We had no idea what was happening in the world outside our trenches—there were no radios on the front lines, and we received no newspapers. We simply did in our set of trenches what we were ordered to do—attack, attack, attack.

We had no water or plumbing in the trenches and considered ourselves fortunate when we had a pit in the frozen ground.

Sometimes we ate frozen food and were thankful to have it. After dark, when fighting was in a lull, the mobile kitchen crew brought a warm meal to a short distance behind the line. One soldier would carry four or five of our kidney-shaped aluminum bowls back to the kitchen and bring our warm supper to us.

When the mobile kitchen came close, the crew also restocked the company bunker with bread, marmalade, cheese, artificial honey, or whatever else had reached the front line. In the bunker, the food was divided for the different groups.

For our group, I often ended up being the one to distribute the cold food. I had a good pocketknife with a blade of mild steel that would handle cutting anything. I soon realized there was another reason my comrades wanted me to divide the food—I was willing to take the last portion.

Rations included cigarettes and, sometimes, liquor made from coal. There were ready takers for my portions. I was thrilled, whenever possible, to exchange them for food.

Orders came for our company to move to another position. I was part of a three-man light machine-gun crew. One of the three carried the gun—about thirty-eight English pounds. The other two each carried two thirty-three-pound cases of ammunition. When marching with the machine gun, I switched the weight from shoulder to shoulder. But carrying the ammunition was a killer—on and on, mile after mile, with unchanging dead weight in each hand.

As evening approached on the endless plain, we marched into a village. The people had adapted to what was available—no trees for miles, but there was mud. The walls of houses were made of sun-dried brick. The roofs were thatched.

Our quartermaster had gone from house to house in the village and selected homes to house us soldiers for the night. The thought of safety crossed my mind. *If some Ukrainians blow up German trains, who's to guarantee the people in this village are our friends?*

The instant I walked into the home where four of us would sleep, warmth hit me. I took off my coat and helmet and was still warm!

The hostess smiled. She and two girls wore drab dresses, aprons, and scarves. The house was one large room with two windows. In one corner was a built-in "box" with an iron door on the end. The box was about eight feet wide, ten feet long, and three feet high. Its walls were made of the same brick as the outside walls of the house. The top appeared to be clay. I'd never seen anything like it.

The host pointed me toward a wash basin. I reached in to wash my hands. The water was warm! I cupped my hands and bathed my face. What a luxury!

The eldest boy spoke broken German. "Glad you come," he translated for his father. "Russia steal our farms. Ukraine want independent. Want be good trade partner with Germany."

As we spoke, a teenage boy brought a sheaf of straw in through the door and headed toward the big "box" in the corner of the room. He opened the door on the end. Inside, fire danced. He added the bundle of straw and closed the door.

When bedtime came, our host pointed to the bed—the clay "box" in the corner. "You sleep," he said through his son.

We soldiers each lay down in our uniforms on the "box." I drifted off to sleep—warm. When morning light shone in the windows, our bed was still warm. The clay had absorbed and held the heat.

That morning, the cold outside felt even colder than usual.

When we arrived at our new position, we grabbed the shovels from the side of our packs, unfolded them, screwed the blade firm, and started digging. After the frozen crust, compared to practice digging in boot camp, digging in the Ukraine was a piece of cake—the soil was rich and dark with a hearty scent. The shovel blade never hit a rock.

Within a few days, my waist itched like crazy. Then I noticed my comrades scratching too.

"Just lice," a veteran soldier explained. "It's the price you pay for a comfortable night sleeping in the homes."

I groaned. "How do you get rid of them?"

"You don't," he sneered. "You name them."

"No, really. How can I get rid of the itching things?"

"Boiling your clothes will kill the adult lice," he said. "But it doesn't hurt the eggs. So, if you see a louse, squash it between your fingernails. Otherwise, ignore them."

"Great," I said. "Another enemy—one that sucks the life out of you and drives you crazy with the itch."

"Yeah," he responded, as nonchalant as if he were talking about balmy weather. "And if he's in a bad mood, he can pass typhus fever on to you."

Morning by morning I washed my face with a handful of snow. Every few days when there was quiet on the front, even though very few bothered with such nonessentials, I moistened my stubble and tore through my whiskers with the dulling razor in my pack. If only I had a clean pair of underwear!

One morning a comrade noticed me taking off my sweater, unbuttoning my shirt, and washing my chest with a handful of snow. "Don't lay your sweater down," he warned.

"Why?" I asked.

"The lice will walk off with it!" He laughed.

I rolled my eyes. "That's about right." I snickered. "Hey, on second thought," I added, "that might be a good bargain—just to be rid of the beasts!"

In the end, the chill won. I pulled the sweater back on.

One night Private Diescht trekked through the darkness to the field kitchen with several of our bowls. As we waited for our warm supper, suddenly we heard laughter, footfalls of a running man, and several gunshots. We readied our guns and listened. Someone was running from the direction of the Russians.

"Don't shoot!" the runner hollered in German. "It's me—Diescht." He slid into our trench, panting.

"What happened?"

"Somehow I missed our trench," he gasped. "I stumbled into one . . . but they were speaking Russian."

"You OK?"

"Yeah. But I dropped our bowls in the scramble to get out."

"Hey, I want my supper," one of the guys joked.

"I'll give you directions," Diescht replied.

We heard the Russians laughing. We joined in.

It felt like an odd camaraderie. Here we were—young men who had nothing against each other; front line soldiers drafted to do a job we didn't want; shooting at each other, killing each other, not because we wanted to but because someone hundreds of miles away had ordered it.

They're just like us, I realized. *Just trying to survive.* Then I wondered, *Who is the enemy anyway?*

While Bullets Fly
1942

Who is the enemy?

It seemed pretty obvious as long as bullets zinged by me and grenades exploded nearby.

Then one morning we were ordered to take a Ukrainian village about half a mile ahead. I fastened my pack. My comrades and I climbed out of our trenches. I picked up two cases of machine-gun ammunition and headed across snow and mud. We started shooting, and the Russian soldiers returned fire. About a third of the way to the village, *boom!*

The explosion slammed me to the ground. I couldn't catch my breath. For an instant I wondered, *Am I alive?*

Indeed. My head pounded. My ears rang. I remembered the order to attack and then setting out on the operation.

Previously we had mined the field. One of my comrades accidentally had tripped a wire to a mine off to my left. Its explosion had thrown me to the ground.

German and Russian machine guns kept firing.

Almost as second nature, I pulled the pack off my shoulders and rolled to my back—less body surface sticking up to catch bullets.

I took stock. Temperature—cold. Just enough above freezing for me to be lying in cold mud. Weather—low overcast. At least for now, it wasn't snowing or raining. Time—midmorning. ID—Georg Grellmann, private in the German army infantry, Alsace-Lorraine Double Cross Division. Date—April 21, 1942, one day after my twentieth birthday. (At least my mind was still working.) Ability to defend myself—no gun or other defense. As part of a three-man machine-gun crew, I'd been carrying ammunition. Body—my left thigh burned white-hot. I wanted to scream with the pain—the scream in my memory of the man whose leg had flown off in Breslau would have to suffice. It would be best not to announce my presence to the Russians.

I slid my head sideways on the ground till I could see my leg—it was there! Red oozed from a hole the size of my thumb in the pant leg over my thigh. *Stop the bleeding,* my training reminded me. I decided to try to reach for my pack and pull out the first-aid kit. When I raised my head an inch, a bullet whistled by. Trusting my body's blood-clotting mechanism more than the generosity of the Russian army, I lay back down and waited.

I was a thousand miles from home. The German army had advanced six hundred miles into the Ukraine. We were east of Kharkov and headed toward Stalingrad. We'd pushed the Russian infantry in the area into retreat. I willed my German comrades to keep the momentum, to take the Ukrainian village half a mile ahead.

Gunfire continued back and forth. Hoping the Russians would assume I was dead and spend their bullets in other directions, I lay motionless, the back of my steel helmet toward the fighting.

Back in the direction from which we'd come, the vast prairie stretched endlessly, no trees anywhere near. An occasional dried up sunflower stalk left over from last year's crop was the biggest interruption to the flat-line horizon.

I shivered—the dampness of the mud chilled me to the bone. But in my thigh, I felt searing heat . . . and the moistness broadening.

If you can't even trust your comrades, whom can you trust? I wondered. *What's life all about anyway? Is this all there is?*

I thought of home and my sweetheart. Hanne and I had promised to be true to each other. But would I see her again? And my brother—how soon would Jo be drafted into this hell? My sister—would Hannchen be able to finish teacher training, or was she stuck in some factory, helping to crank out weapons? Mutti and Vater—would they be safe? How would they hear about my being wounded or—my breath caught—about my demise?

Eventually, the changes of the gunfire told me my comrades had advanced. I turned my head. As far as I could tell, everyone was in or near the village. I pulled the first-aid kit out of my pack, grabbed a bandage, and inched upward. No bullets came my direction. I sat up. Blood had stained my pant leg wide around the hole. The bleeding had probably slowed by now. I bandaged the wound and then lay back down.

The afternoon dragged by. My leg swelled. It throbbed with every heartbeat, exploded in pain with every movement. The questions I'd asked about the man who'd lost his leg so many years before came alive and personal. I thought of things I enjoyed—bicycling, hiking, swimming, ice-skating, skiing. *Will I never be able to do any of them again?* And I thought about work—an oral surgeon stands all day. *Will I be able to stand? Will I be able to work? To support a family?* I thought about love—*Will Hanne reject me if I lose a leg?* The thought sent a shiver up my spine.

Cold also gripped every cell of my body. The shooting sounded as though it was in or beyond the village. In late afternoon, the firing stopped.

Finally, at dusk, I heard the *clop, clop, clop* of horse hooves, then the varying whistle of sleigh runners on snow, then mud, then snow. I spotted the horse and two men surveying the battlefield. *Friend or foe?* I wondered.

A sigh escaped when I finally could make out the outline of German boots. "Over here!" I called, loud enough for the horse and rescue crew to hear, quiet enough not to broadcast my position to a broad audience.

They turned toward me. I waved. "Over here."

The rescuers waved back. The horse pulled the back of the sleigh up beside my head. The medics leaned over me. "How bad is your injury?" one asked.

"A mine got my leg," I responded. "I can still move it, but it hurts like crazy. The bleeding has stopped."

They took a look at the wound and then rebandaged my leg. "How about a sleigh ride?" one quipped.

It was really a sledge, a poor excuse for a sleigh. It consisted of two parallel poles with boards between them. The poles extended beyond the boards on each end. The front rode a little higher than the horse's knees, while the rear of the poles dragged on the ground.

The field medics hoisted me headfirst onto the wood sled. "How'd the battle go?" I asked.

One of them gave me a thumbs-up. "We took the village!" He strapped me onto the sled then added, "This isn't apt to be the most comfortable ride you've ever had, but at least we shouldn't have to deal with enemy fire while we get you to help."

"Gid-up," his partner urged the horse. "Easy."

We hadn't moved five feet when one of the poles dropped into a hole. "Ouch!" I moaned.

"Sorry," one said. "And it won't get any better for quite a ways."

He was right about that! We bumped over the prairie. With each jostle—and the jostles were almost continuous—pain jabbed up and down my leg. With each bump, pain exploded through me. "How far?" I asked.

"About three miles to the medic tent."

"And no roads," the other one added. "It's rough."

I breathed deeply, trying to focus on something other than the pain, *anything* other than the pain!

I listened to the regular rhythm of the horse's *clop, clop, clop*. I looked for stars—no luck in the cloudy skies. But I searched anyway, since looking for stars was still better than revisiting the memory of the bicyclist whose leg went flying.

I tried to be quiet, but, with the bigger bumps, a moan escaped from time to time. And when one pole or both dropped into a trench or other hole, I wanted to scream.

Clop, clop, clop. Ouch, ouch, *ow-w-w*!

Reaching the medics' tent was a welcome relief! With the light of a kerosene lamp, a medic removed the bandage from my leg and tore the hole in my pant leg larger. He examined the wound then called for something. Another medic came with a syringe. "I'll deaden the area of the wound," the medic said.

After the injection, his assistant handed him a scalpel, and he began trimming away mangled tissue around the hole in my leg.

Other medics worked over other men. Moans filled the tent. I worried as they worked. As they rebandaged my leg, I asked, "Will I lose my leg?"

The medic threw back his head. He and his assistants laughed heartily. "Kid," the medic said, his voice more sympathetic again, "I know it hurts like all get out, but you're going to be fine."

I sighed deeply. I didn't much like the pain, but I could stand it. As long as I could keep my leg, I would be fine.

I heard a truck drive up. The medics loaded the wounded on their canvas litters onto the canvas-covered truck bed.

We bumped over the first few miles. I felt every pothole we dropped into, but it wasn't too bad for me at first. Then the anesthetic around my wound started wearing off.

"How long in this truck?" I asked the medic who was aiding a moaning man near me.

"Five or six hours," he said, "if things go well and there are no enemy planes."

The ride was torture. My leg throbbed. Pain jabbed me with

every bump and exploded in my leg with every pothole. But I also rejoiced. When it seemed as though I couldn't stand the pain anymore, I refocused on breathing deeply and told myself, *I get to keep my leg! I get to keep my leg! I'm one of the lucky ones.*

I felt sorry for the severely wounded men around me. Some moaned until the pain became more than their bodies could bear, and they lost consciousness.

Breathe deeply, I told myself. *Get your mind off the pain.* But the truck rolled on. Bounce, bounce, lurch. Ouch, ouch, *ow-w-w!*

Chapter 13

Return
1942

Finally, in the darkness, our truck came to a stop. The wounded were loaded into a train, and it headed west. My leg still hurt, but the rails were significantly smoother than the potholes of the dirt roads the truck had traveled.

Two days later the train chugged through Koenigsberg. I scanned the streets, looking for the university I would attend someday. As soon as we finished fighting this war, I would go to *gymnasium* then to the university on scholarship and become an oral surgeon. How I longed for the war to end, to have no battlefields, to get on with life. I didn't see the university, but it didn't stop me from dreaming.

Through the day we crossed Germany. What a relief to be back on German soil! Spring flowers were starting to bloom in the valleys. That evening we arrived at a hospital in Engen in southwest Germany. Female nurses swarmed the place. One was going to help me with a bath.

Shy and embarrassed by my lack of hygiene, I begged, "Isn't there a man who can help me? Please?"

They finally agreed to send for one. An elderly man came. In no time, my clothing was stripped and my left leg propped up on a chair. The rest of me was in a tub of water—*warm* water.

"I'm sorry," I started, "about the dirt . . ."

"Soldier, don't you worry!" A small smile ruffled his wrinkles. "I remember what the battlefield felt like in World War I. And I remember getting clean when it was all over. You just relax. Enjoy it!"

I felt my shoulder muscles relax. I leaned back against the edge of the tub and soaked in the warmth.

Before long I was scrubbed clean, shaved close, and resting between clean sheets in a comfortable bed with blankets! A clerk helped me prepare a telegram to my parents. Then I slept—no mortars, no machine guns, no mines, no potholes in the road, no swaying of the train.

The next morning, after a dressing change on my wound, an attractive young lady came to my bedside. "Greetings," she said cheerily. "My name is Erika. I came to thank you for what you've done for our country." She placed a big bouquet of fragrant peonies on the stand beside my bed then handed me a box with a ribbon. "A gift for you," she offered.

I opened the box. It was full of chocolate and other candies—treats I hadn't seen in months.

"Th-thank you," I stammered, still looking at the treats.

"Go ahead," she said. "Give them a try."

Chocolate melted in my mouth, its sweetness awaking dormant taste buds. It brought back memories—so many memories. It reminded me of a world that had become a distant memory.

Erika interrupted my reverie. "Looks like you enjoy chocolate."

I smiled. "*Ja*. Reminds me of home. Chocolate was the special treat Vater would get for special occasions."

"Where is home?" she asked.

"Breslau," I replied. "My girlfriend lives there too." The female attention felt good, but I wanted this young woman to know right away that I had a girlfriend.

"Wonderful," she enthused. "Tell me about her."

We talked about Hanne and home until Erika eventually said, "I've got to get home and help ·Mutter. You have a good day. Be good to that leg so it can heal up quickly."

My brother Jo showed up at my bedside late that afternoon. It was great to see him! He barely had begun to catch me up on the news from home when Erika arrived again. She was just as friendly to him. In fact, she invited him to stay at her family's home while he visited me. When Jo left a couple days later and Mutti arrived, Erika invited her, also, to stay at her family's home.

What a treat to see family! To hear Mutti's voice. To wear clean clothes! To be served *warm* food! And to get it at regular intervals!

After Jo and Mutti left for home, Erika still visited regularly. She assured me that my fighting in the military contributed to defeating the enemy—Communism. "I am sure you have heard this before," she said, "but don't forget what an honor it is to fight on the Russian front."

Yes, I had heard it before . . . when they gave us our orders to head to Russia. But after six months on the front line, it didn't feel like much of an honor.

With ointment, dressing changes, and one cauterizing treatment, my wound healed quickly. Soon, in spite of pain deep in my leg, I got around with crutches. Sometimes I took the train a short distance to Konstanz, Lindau, or Radolfzell. In Konstanz, Martin Luther had stood trial. Near Lindau the giant Zeppelins had been designed and built. Radolfzell had interesting shops. I looked for a gift for Hanne. Nothing seemed quite right until I found a beautifully carved, small wooden box with inlaid roses of a deep red-colored wood. It was expensive but exquisite.

Should I spend that much?

Ja, I decided. *Now I can give her a gift. If I don't come home, she will know forever I loved her. Besides, if I do survive, it is a fitting gift for the woman with whom I will enjoy the rest of my life.*

When my wound had healed closed, I swam in Lake Bodensee, propelling myself with one leg. I looked forward to the time I could use both legs normally and swim, hike, or ski with my friends. Sometimes I looked across the lake to Switzerland and wondered about her stance as a neutral nation.

After about three weeks, though my leg still hurt, and there was a hard lump under the scar, I could get around without crutches. A doctor said I could leave the hospital, and the clerk dated my soldier's passbook for a three-week home leave. I sent a telegram—"Home Thursday." Then I grabbed my few belongings and headed for the train station, making sure my passbook was in my pocket.

The small booklet was my constant companion. As my identification, it included my name, address, blood group, troop, and military home base—Idar-Oberstein. When I wasn't on active duty, the passbook was stamped with the date I had to return. It also opened up free travel on any public transportation. The 550-mile trip home was pleasant. My uniform prompted smiles and grateful comments from strangers. Hopes were obviously high. Patriotism was strong.

As the train neared Breslau, my heart raced with excitement. I took the tram straight home—gazing at the oft-seen sights, enjoying even the familiar click-clacking as the tram's overhead connectors changed lines. I spotted our apartment house. Then I was at our door. I had barely opened the door when Mutti hurried from the kitchen—her eyes glistening.

After the greeting, I dropped my bag on my bed. I reached into the bag and ran a finger over the wood of my gift for Hanne. *I get to see her!* I thought. *Soon!* My heart beat a little faster. "Mutti," I ventured, "would you like to see the gift I brought Hanne?"

"*Ja.* Certainly."

I pulled the box out of my bag and held it out toward Mutti.

She gasped. Her eyes got big. She touched the smooth wood. "It's beautiful, Georg!"

"Do you think she will like it?"

"*Ja, ja,*" she said. "Very much. It is very beautiful."

I told her about looking for a special gift then finding the shop of the artist who had carved this box.

"How much did it cost you?" Mutti asked.

I told her.

She sucked in her breath. "How could you spend nearly a month's wages for a gift?"

"I'd rather spend it now," I said, "than to be unable to give anything. Now it gives me pleasure to give her something beautiful. Who knows what the future holds?"

Mutti swallowed hard and nodded, a tear welling up in one eye.

Soon, Jo came home from school. The three of us chattered through supper together. Vater had taken a bookkeeping class and gotten a job in Auerbach in the state of Saxony. He was working there and would be home for the weekend. Hannchen was at teacher training. Hanne was working at a hospital and would be at her home after supper.

It felt wonderful to be home!

It also felt wonderful to take the tram to see Hanne, to climb the steps to her family's apartment, to ring her doorbell. For an instant, when she opened the door, we just stood there, looking into each other's eyes. All the warmth I remembered was there. We fell into each other's arms.

Three weeks was *way* too short. Hannchen got to come home over one Sabbath. Going to church and seeing my friends was a special delight. In the little time I had, it seemed that everyone wanted to spoil me. Hanne and I talked about getting engaged and decided to talk to our parents about it. Hanne's mother seemed pleased, but her father was somewhat concerned. My parents had reservations, too, but didn't want to discourage me. I sensed they were thinking that if we got engaged now and I came home again, we'd probably want to get married. What if Hanne got pregnant, and then I was killed in the war?

We decided to go ahead. I made two simple gold rings—Hanne and I thought they would protect our relationship in the eyes of others. We had a quiet engagement celebration dinner at our house with Hanne and her parents.

All too quickly, the three weeks melted away. My leg had improved so I didn't limp, unless I walked quite a bit. The lump under the scar had not shrunk and, when I walked very much, the pain grew severe. I said my goodbyes and took the train to my original base in Alsace-Lorraine. I showed the hard lump to the doctor.

"Just a mine splinter," he snorted. "A little metal in your leg won't keep you from shooting a gun!" He wrote on my chart and then looked up. "Ready for duty," he snapped.

The clerk gave me orders to ship to the big base in Idar-Oberstein. There, first thing, I went to see another doctor. "Please, do something,"

Georg in the army shortly after he was wounded

I begged. "If I walk very much my leg becomes painful. If I go back to the battlefront like this, I will put my comrades in danger."

He examined my leg and agreed. At the army hospital, a surgeon removed a mine splinter about half the size of my thumb. It had penetrated to the bone.

My leg healed quickly, and I was assigned to a new company.

*   *   *

Back in the Ukraine, we advanced, and Ivan retreated, but our losses were high at first. When it was quiet at night, we buried our dead comrades. After a couple of weeks, battle fatalities dropped drastically. Thinking back, I realized the same thing had happened when my initial division reached the battlefield. I thought about other companies that had come. It seemed true for them too. Were soldiers less careful when they first arrived? Did they think they were invincible? Were their minds preoccupied with thoughts of home? *There can't be an unguarded second,* I concluded.

One night I mentioned my observation to a veteran comrade in a trench. *"Ja,"* he agreed, "whether you're a newcomer or coming back from home leave, you're more likely to get killed the first two or three weeks than any other time."

A few nights later I heard celebration. "What's that?" I asked the same veteran comrade.

"Time for high alert," he said.

"Why?"

"When Ivan celebrates, they have been given vodka. They will attack soon."

After the battle, we buried friend and foe. The fighting, the wounds, the death made me think, *Futility!* I dared not focus on futility very long, or I wouldn't be alert enough to keep myself alive. A comrade's earlier words played again through my mind—*"Just do what you have to do to try to survive."* That and follow orders! I thought.

For now, the orders were "Hold the position." I set my mind to doing so.

Germans and Russians weren't alone on the battlefield. Others had joined German troops to fight Communism—near us were an Italian division, a small contingent of volunteers from England and France, and a company of Cossacks.

We fought on and on. Kiev fell. Kharkov changed hands twice. Our division was involved in fighting in the Donezk area, including towns such as Saporoshje, Dnepropetrovsk, Poltava, and Kremenchug. We pushed forward steadily toward Stalingrad, eager to win the war and get home.

Civilians deserted their villages as fighting approached. Homes looked occupied, but no one was around. Schools were quiet. Churches that had been vacated decades earlier were filled with farm equipment and supplies.

Someone must have observed that I was good with directions. I was called to the company commander. He reassigned me to be a messenger, along with another comrade. We drew sketches of the front line, including positions of enemy weapons—machine guns, snipers, grenade throwers, artillery, etc. At night we carried our drawings and messages back and forth between the front line and the outpost command center. Nights with no moon were dangerous because we couldn't see. Nights with moonlight were more dangerous because we could be seen.

Our sense of hearing was critical. We identified the lines in various ways. Firing patterns were different—for instance, the Italian division near us tended to shoot incessantly. The sounds of weapons varied. Even though I couldn't hear words, I recognized the language of the sound.

Instinctively, we learned what fire was aimed at us. The sniper was one of the most deadly. At night Ivan often used tracer ammunition. We especially feared the type of bullets that exploded on impact, causing big wounds.

One day I was walking with no cover or foxhole. Suddenly I heard the whine of the Stalin Organ. I hit the ground. Like carpet bombing, Stalin Organ fire was calculated to hit you no matter where you dropped—large numbers of grenades blanketed an area leaving no undamaged space between explosions. Often, a phosphoric substance was added into the shells. It increased the likelihood of fire and, when it hit a person, poisoned the wounds.

The grinding sound flew my direction. My heart raced. Grenades exploded around me. Then stacks of straw bundles a few feet from me in different directions burst into flame.

I couldn't believe I hadn't been hit. I dared not move for fear the enemy would spot me. I dared not stay in this stubble field for fear of the fires that surrounded me.

I lay still, feeling the heat from the burning straw bundles. I watched to determine what path the fire would take toward me. Strangely, the dry stubble in which I was lying did not catch fire. *Why?* I wondered.

*   *   *

One day I had to march twenty prisoners of war back from the front line. As we passed a field, one turned to me with pleading eyes. He pointed to the field and then to his mouth. I looked at the crop—cabbage. Some were damaged, some undamaged. The other prisoners were watching. I nodded. All twenty scattered into the edge of the field, scooped up cabbage heads in their arms, and ate as though they were starving. When they quit eating cabbage, we moved on. *When did they last eat? I wondered. And what will they get to eat in our captivity? What will happen to them?*

Another night while determining positions, my fellow messenger and I spotted two Russian scouts before they spotted us. Silently, we trained our rifles on them. "Halt!" my partner shouted. In one fluid movement, the Russian soldiers gasped, dropped their guns, and raised their hands in surrender. We confiscated their weapons and marched them behind our line.

Nighttime flares were another danger. Women piloted most of the small Russian planes we called sewing machines. Vulnerable during daytime, they flew at night, often dropping flares to light up the ground. With a flare, we had to freeze—any movement would give us away, and then a bomb would be released.

Sometimes at night the pilots of those planes would turn off the engine. They would glide silently while using listening devices.

When the front line stabilized, civilians would return to their villages that were within a few miles of the battlefront. One night I was ordered to go through a village to remind anyone whose lights showed of the protection of blackout—Russian airplanes might bomb any place that was lighted up. Walking by a home, I saw a tiny faint glint on the top of one window frame. I stepped up to the door and raised my hand to knock. Just then I heard a familiar melody, as if it was whispered in singing.

I couldn't understand the Russian words, but the German words played in my mind: "O God, our help in ages past, / Our hope for years to come. . . ." I stood awestruck at this evidence of faith in a country where religion had been outlawed for longer than I had lived.

My hand dropped to my side. I couldn't bring myself to interrupt their worship. *I can barely see the spot of light,* I thought. *And it is only visible from below the window. No one in a plane will see it.* I listened to the music for a minute more and then turned and walked on. *Will God honor their trust?* I wondered. *Will He honor my own mother's prayers?*

Predictions
1942

Sometimes when the front line stabilized for any length of time, mail would be delivered to the troops. I might get two or three letters from Mutti and the same from Hanne. Mutti's letters were filled with news:

> Rudi was sent to the Russian front recently. The church misses his trumpet playing. Sabbath the organist said she missed your pumping the bellows for her. Said you always gave her nice, even air which made her playing sound better.
>
> Jo was baptized last week. He will graduate in two weeks. I'm sure a draft notice will soon follow. When it does, I'll join Vater in Auerbach, Saxony.
>
> I know it must not be possible, but if you can send mail out, we'd surely love to hear from you.
>
> I pray for you many times a day. God will be your refuge and strength. Remember Psalm 46?

> God is our refuge and strength, a very present help in trouble. Therefore will not we fear, though the earth be removed, and though the mountains be carried into the midst of the sea; though the waters thereof roar and be

troubled, though the mountains shake with the swelling thereof (verses 1–3).

The Lord of hosts is with us; the God of Jacob is our refuge (verse 11).

We are looking forward to seeing you. We pray the war will end soon, and you'll be home!

Love,
Mutti

Hanne's letters were filled with dreams. They assured me of her love and reminded me of our plans. They gave me fodder for dreaming for many a long night.

We pushed south during the peak of summer—from hot to hotter. From Kertsch on the broad Crimea peninsula into the Black Sea, we crossed the Straight of Kertsch in small boats. The breeze from moving over water felt refreshing. In the distance, the snowcapped Caucasus Mountains jutted their peaks into blue sky. On the far shore, sunlight highlighted a village of white houses. The buildings, made from cut blocks of white coral, seemed to glow. The beauty startled me. It stood in stark contrast to the ugliness of war.

The village, shining in the sun, reminded me of artist's paintings of the New Jerusalem. I stood on the bow of the boat mesmerized by the peaceful scene.

When we hit shore, there was no more time for reflection. We headed east again by foot and took up our position along the Kuban River. Days in the swamps were unbearably hot and humid. We shared our trenches with scorpions three inches long. They were friends, however, compared to the mosquitoes—swarms of them, feasting on us continually, each bite bearing the threat of malaria.

After a few weeks in the swamps, medics came through the trenches regularly, checking for fever. Sometimes no one left with them, sometimes many.

At night every soldier had to be at his post. During the day, some of us could try to get some sleep, unless we were advancing or withdrawing. Then no one got any sleep.

One day a corporal came through the trenches handing out a new type of grenade launcher and telling us how to use it. Late that afternoon I decided to test it. "The grenade will arc high like a miniature grenade thrower," he had told us. "Aiming is pure guesswork, but if you hold the barrel of your gun straight up, the grenade will come straight back down and get you." I stood my rifle in the trench, fixed the attachment at the end of the barrel, and slid the slender grenade—about four inches long and one inch in diameter—into the attachment. I leaned the rifle far enough to the side so that the grenade would not hit our lines. Then I inserted the cartridge that would shoot the grenade off and let it fly.

I reached to dismantle the attachment, satisfied that I knew how to use this new weapon when I would get into a situation where it would be the best weapon as I fought for my life.

A scream pierced the stillness. The grenade must have fallen directly into Ivan's trench.

Sadness welled up within me. I had hurt someone needlessly. Guilt needled me. I couldn't help thinking of the Jehovah's Witness man who chose to be shot rather than inflict injury on another. *What about all the grenades, bullets, and bombs?* I wondered. *All the wounded? All the dead and dying? Is it all needless?*

Nights grew long while we listened and watched. The more I tried to understand all the fighting, the more frustrating it became. It made no sense. I often escaped into dreaming about a better future. If it were cloudless, I would look up to the stars and moon and think of my sweetheart.

Then there was fighting again. We Germans feared becoming prisoners of Ivan. I had heard many a comrade say, "Save your last bullet for yourself."

In a way, it was better when there was a lot of activity. When we were fighting, we tried to survive. Our training shifted into gear, and fighting was second nature. Action gave us less time to think about our situation.

The heat of summer finally gave way to autumn—wet, cold, miserable. A bad case of diarrhea hit the ranks. Exhaustion and casualties increased.

One day my comrade messenger and I were sent on an errand. Returning through a deserted village, I saw a broom lying on the street and took it along to sweep our bunker. As we walked, Ivan watched us. Since we were out of range for most of their weapons, we didn't worry.

Then we heard artillery being shot off. Suddenly alert, we looked to see if it was coming our way. Yes! We flattened ourselves to the ground. Just in front of me, a grenade hit and made a crater.

As the dust settled, the advice of World War I stories hit me. "If a grenade hits and makes a crater, jump into it. No grenades will hit the same spot twice."

I started to push up so I could jump into the crater. But a new salvo of grenades came down on us. I flattened myself again. As I lay there, I saw a second grenade hit the center of the first crater and blow it deeper.

Was it just luck that I didn't have time to jump? I wondered. *Or is God answering my family's prayers?*

Day or night there was always sporadic shooting. Bullets whizzed by. It was just part of life. If we drew aimed fire, I ran, but not at night or if I knew I was out of reach. At times the enemy trenches were close to ours. We could even hear each other talk.

When our trenches ran along the river or in certain areas where the ground water level was high, we couldn't dig deep enough to walk upright. On my errands, I jumped across places in the trench where water had collected.

One day as I bounced over a puddle, a bullet whistled past my nose. Apparently Ivan's snipers had noticed the spots where heads sometimes bobbed above the surface. For fun, I grabbed the broom I'd brought earlier. Over the puddle, I thrust the broom head upward, so the bristles showed slightly. Ivan promptly responded by shooting the bristles off with his machine gun. "Well," I told the comrade beside me, "that bullet won't get you or me!"

When we thought there could be nothing worse than autumn along the Kuban River, winter came. Everywhere we stepped or put our hands, there was mud. The dampness chilled us to the bone. When I could find clean straw, I changed the straw in my boots—every autumn I tried to get oversized boots and then surrounded my feet with straw for insulation. We had worn the same clothes—including underwear—for several months. We cracked lice between our thumbnails. Sometimes Ivan and we moved in the same field just a hundred yards apart, but neither had the heart to shoot at the other.

Sometimes dreaming of better days could take my mind off the moment. These conditions got so depressing that thinking of home, of decent food, and of a cozy bed was overpowering.

One winter day another comrade and I got an order that sent us from the trenches to the hinterland. Snow covered the ground. The air was bitter. A village only a couple miles from the front line was nearly deserted, but smoke curled up from one chimney. "Let's go to that house and warm up," I suggested.

We knocked. An elderly man opened the door. He looked at us, up and down the street, then back at us. "Welcome," he said, motioning us in.

We stamped the snow off our boots. Warmth drew us in.

In the light of the one small window, I saw that several women and elderly men filled the room. A middle-aged woman spoke in broken German, "Stove here. Come warm." A couple of elderly men scooted their chairs sideways to make room by the stove and motioned us to join them.

We tore off our mittens, unbuttoned our coats, and held our hands out toward the stove. My fingers tingled as they started to warm. I squeezed them—right hand, left hand, right—trying to ease the discomfort. Although it hurt my thawing hands, the warmth felt cozy and safe.

We'd barely thawed the outer layer when the German speaker said, "On battlefront, you two must wonder about future." She reached out to my comrade. "Let me see palm. I tell you what happen."

He pushed his hand toward her.

Focusing on his palm, she said, "You married. You have one daughter."

He glanced over at me, creases lining his brow.

My heart pounded. Experiences and stories flashed through my mind—little black beings in our childhood bedroom, knocking on our kitchen and bedroom windows, a spiritualist hypnotizing people, and my mother's Bible picked up and thrown across the room. This woman could not know this information on her own, and it wasn't from heaven.

The woman kept right on. "At home you work in coal mine."

"How do you know all that?" my partner asked her.

"It's in your palm," she responded. She told him he would go home safely but would have to find a new job. Then she turned to me. "Give me your palm," she invited.

I shook my head. "No."

Surprise registered on her face. Then she smiled. "I do not need palm," she said. She looked me in the eye and spoke. "You have one sister and one brother. And a girlfriend. You live to be . . ."

"We will go now," I announced.

Everyone in the room looked up at me, shock in their eyes.

I would leave my future up to God. I didn't want to hear any predictions from the enemy. I glanced out the window at the snow. *No matter how cold it is out there, I am not staying here.*

"Thank you for letting us warm up," I said. I grabbed my coat and headed for the door.

CHAPTER 15

When You Are Here
1943

On the front line, we didn't know what was happening anywhere other than within sight or hearing distance of our trench.
We heard rumors that our troops had progressed to Stalingrad and
that sections of submarines were on the way to be reassembled at
the Caspian Sea as soon as we could reach it. Even as a messenger,
I was involved only with local placements and strategies. Still, for
the last few months, it was clear we weren't moving with the earlier
momentum.

One morning when Russian airplanes cruised above our positions,
higher than we could reach with any firepower we had, something
unusual fell from one of the planes. Whatever it was, it broke apart
and fell slowly, as snow on a still day.

Shortly, a storm of leaflets fell over the German side of the battlefield. Bold letters announced in German, *"Freihes Deutschland!"*—"A
Free Germany!"

The main article said that German General Paulus had surrendered
Stalingrad and agreed that Russia will assist in forming a new and free
Germany.

The logic seemed absurd. *Germany is free,* I thought. Then, on second thought, *It isn't exactly our personal choice to be on this front line,*

but then every country has its armies to protect themselves. Considering the demonstrations I'd seen as a child, the stories I'd heard earlier from Poland and during this war from Ukrainians, the thought of Communist Russia helping create freedom seemed ludicrous. Besides, Germany had already gained victory across a thousand miles of Russia.

Some in the trenches guessed there surely was no truth in the Russian leaflets—"just enemy propaganda." I wanted to believe it. Yet, lately, when we lost a tank, it wasn't replaced. We saw German planes less and less. And several times recently, when replacement troops arrived, it appeared they hadn't been trained well.

The front line was in flux. We changed positions so frequently that we had no time to dig continuous trenches. We used only foxholes. The advantage we had held for years seemed to have turned to Ivan. And Ivan became more daring.

More often than not we withdrew, and lately we had less and less weaponry. For the best protection we had at that point, we placed a machine gun on an elevated point, giving it commanding angles. One night I heard a hand grenade explode nearby, followed by a scuffle. By the time I got there, the struggle was over. The machine gunner trembled in a foxhole. He had heard a sound and started to aim toward it. It was too late. The machine gun was pulled away from him, and he dropped into a foxhole. Ivan took off with the German machine gunner's assistant and the machine gun.

Occasionally, through the war, headquarters ordered a commando to capture a man from the other side and bring him back alive. The chances of surviving the assignment were so low the comrades called it *ein Himmelfahrts Kommando*—an ascension order to heaven.

One day I got the dreaded order. I was to join two wireless operators, two other comrades, and a lieutenant for the operation. I had never seen the lieutenant before, and those of his rank weren't usually sent on such commando raids. Something looked fishy.

One of the wireless operators knew more—"This is punishment for him," he whispered, "and an opportunity to redeem himself."

That made the rest of us all the more nervous. We hated to go into enemy territory with someone who wasn't accustomed to front line combat, and especially one who had proved himself unreliable enough to receive such punishment. But . . . orders are orders.

After dark, we headed into no-man's-land, then held back to see how the lieutenant would lead. He had gone behind a tree. He was so terrified he had messed his trousers.

We knew we couldn't depend on him. Relieved, we moved ahead without him. I never saw him again.

Ivan had also sent out a scouting patrol. Fortunately, we noticed them before they spotted us. We captured two and made it safely back to our line.

Afterward, I learned more about the new troops on our right flank, most of whom were older than the rank and file of the front line troops. They had all been officers, pilots, or captains of submarines. Each, trying to look good in the eyes of their superiors, had filed false reports and been found out. For punishment, they had been sent to fight on the Russian front.

Punishment? my mind screamed. *PUNISHMENT? So, if it is punishment for them to fight on the Russian front, how is it an* honor *for the rest of us?*

My thoughts broiled. I didn't dare voice them, but I couldn't help noticing in others a lift of an eyebrow, a drop of a jaw, or the slightest inflection of suspicion. I wasn't the only one who wondered.

The swarms of mosquitoes didn't help our attitude. The medics kept busy checking for malaria. One night when a medic came by and felt my forehead, he pulled out his thermometer and stuck it under my armpit. Not a good sign. When he looked at the thermometer, there was no question in his voice. "You're heading out now."

That night I marched four miles to the next medical tent—along with several others from our outfit. The next day, those of us who had malaria were transported by truck to a small harbor. Russian planes would attack the ferries during the day, so we waited there till nightfall to be ferried across to the Crimea.

On the ferry ride, I suddenly felt chilled and began to shake. I crawled onto the truck bed and lay down. My teeth chattered. My head began to ache. I shook so severely I could hardly catch my breath. I felt sure I was going to die.

Later they told me the shaking lasted about twenty minutes. It felt like twenty hours. Afterward every cell in my body felt exhausted. I'd barely gotten over the chill when I began to feel hot—way *too* hot.

The ferry finally made land. The truck bumped to a makeshift hospital. The medic took my temperature. He raised his eyebrows. "Forty-two degrees," he said. That was centigrade—it was 106 degrees Fahrenheit.

I didn't care what scale they used . . . or if I lived or died.

A medic gave me a shot. In a couple hours I started sweating, and my temperature dropped to normal. But I didn't feel normal. I didn't know it was possible to feel more exhausted than I had after the shaking. It was. I slept, except for when they came by with their hypodermic needles.

By late afternoon, I started to feel human again. Shortly after sunset, I began to shake. It got every bit as bad as the night before. Chattering and shaking, I made sure I was at peace with God and then waited to die. But eventually I quit shaking, and my fever spiked again.

Two days in a row just after sunset I'd gone through the same paroxysms. The third day I hated to see the sun closing down on the horizon.

Sure enough, just after sunset, I began to shake. I followed the same course as the nights before.

On the fourth day, I was dreading to see the sun go down. But the shaking didn't come. After a few days the symptoms and the dread disappeared, and I was ferried and marched back to the front line.

For a while, one of my duties was to make sketches of the front line and mark where we knew Ivan had a machine gun, a sniper, a T-34 tank, and the heavier weapons farther back from the front line. That took me to other companies and battalions within our regiment. When I returned to my own company after my second time gone, one of my comrades said, "Grellmann, it goes bad when you are gone. You should stay here."

I snickered. *As if I have any impact on how things go for the unit,* I thought.

But several times different comrades said the same thing. After one trip, an officer reassigned me. "Grellmann," he said, "things go better when you are here."

I was puzzled. *Is it true?* I wondered. *How can it be?*

The officer paused only a moment. My attention snapped back to what he was saying. "You will stay and write the letters to the next of kin of fallen comrades."

"*Ja,* sir," I responded. Mentally I groaned. I would have chosen almost any other mission. But it was an assignment. I began writing letters—"We regret to inform you . . ."

Some days there were few letters to write, sometimes many. I couldn't help picturing the sadness of parents, sweethearts, and children. And I couldn't help wondering if someone someday would write a similar letter to my family.

One day sixteen comrades from another unit joined ours.

"Sure seems like if the army can find us to replace the dead, they ought to be able to find us to deliver some mail," grumbled a comrade.

"Indeed," complained another. "I haven't seen mail in weeks!"

No one in our division had. I longed for a letter from Hanne. Sometimes when I had a chance, I looked at her photo and dreamed. Even a letter from Mutti would cheer me.

That night as I walked down a trench, I stopped in amazement. "Gerhard?" I whispered.

The soldier looked directly at me. His eyes brightened. "Georg?" he asked in a hushed voice. "Is that you?"

"*Ja,*" I said. "I haven't seen you since boot camp. Where have you been?"

"Battling across the Ukraine," he whispered. "We lost most of our company. They brought us survivors here."

"What do you hear of the war?" I asked.

"We lost Stalingrad," he responded. "And thousands of men."

I thought I heard a straw break. We looked silently into the darkness and listened for a long time. Nothing came of the sound.

When Gerhard eventually whispered again, he was reflective. "War is hell." I heard him take several deep breaths. "But, then, things weren't easy back home in Breslau either," he continued. "Mutter and Vater fought all the time. Vater was religious and always wanted to cram religion into my head. Mutter was an atheist and argued for all she was worth that there was no God. I followed after her. But sometimes I wonder." Gerhard paused long. "Grellmann, do you really believe . . ." He looked into the night sky. "Do you really believe there is a God . . . somewhere . . . out there behind the stars?"

"*Ja . . .*" I started.

I didn't know what to say. He knew I believed there was a God. Gerhard could be friendly. And he could be fun. But he could also be very sarcastic. Did I want to risk the bile he might spew at me?

I don't remember what I said. I needed to get back to my position, so, after we finished our whispered conversation, I headed on down the trench.

The next morning, I was the first to be wading the trenches. In the half-light, I nearly stepped on Gerhard. He was lying there . . . blood all over. A grenade had blown the side of his head away.

Writing to Gerhard's parents was horrible. I vowed I would visit them when I went home to Breslau . . . *if* I ever went home.

After darkness that night, we buried Gerhard. But I couldn't get him out of my mind. *What did I say to him that night? What should I have said to him? Did he make peace with God? What do I believe in my heart of hearts? What would I say if someone else asked me such a question?*

Trust
1943

Ivan dropped leaflets more frequently.

What should we believe? I wondered. From history class, I knew Russia had changed sides before. They had gladly taken half of Poland at the beginning of the war, but even then it was clear in Germany that Hitler felt some intrigue was going on behind the scenes between Russia and the western allies. Why should we believe anything the Russians wrote?

On the other hand, to us soldiers on the Russian front, Germany had denied having to surrender Stalingrad for weeks after the fact. And I had followed orders that seemed ludicrous to soldiers on that part of the front line. I was suspicious of information from either side, but some of the articles in the leaflets coincided with the ground I knew we were losing.

Ivan kept right on our heels as we began to withdraw from the Caucasus. We withdrew nearly to the Straight of Asov with no sign of boats or ferries to deliver us from a fate worse than death. We dug in and held our line for several days. Still, no indication of rescue. Would our command sacrifice us?

We kept holding on by sheer willpower. The Russians had plenty of firepower. We were running out of ammunition. Our food was gone. I wondered if I would shortly be missing in action or if Hanne and my family would be alerted of my fate.

Finally, one night we heard boats. Ours was the next-to-last regiment to leave the bridgehead in the Caucasus. When we reached Crimea, we were put onto JU-52 planes—the workhorses of the German army. We were flown someplace in the center of the Russian front line, disembarked onto an open field, and then we were ordered to dig in and stop Ivan where he had broken through. Shortly the enemy appeared. To survive meant to fight. Ivan felt more resistance than they'd expected and also dug in.

Later we learned that fresh SS troops—Hitler's carefully trained Elite Guard—had arrived at the Russian front, had been attacked, and had given way. At this point in the war, German troops dreaded an assignment to the Russian front and had little fighting spirit left. In comparison, we who had fought there from the beginning were not so ready to give way under attack. The Russian high command noted that and focused their attacks on fresh troops.

Ivan also used tactics we had used on them earlier—they concentrated armament and troops on one point. They tried to break through with tanks, follow them with swarms of infantry, and go as far and fast as they could, thus forcing the rest of the front line back.

For months as we retreated across the Ukraine, we saw no German tanks. Ivan, on the other hand, got more of everything. Increasing numbers of American planes flew in the skies—our rifle bullets could do them no harm! Nobody dared say it aloud, but we all knew we were losing the war. One comrade muttered, "I wish we could lock up Stalin, Hitler, Churchill, and Roosevelt in a room together to fight this out between them and let us go home!"

"*Ja!*" everyone agreed.

Russian deserters no longer crossed over to us. We hardly ever took any prisoners. Occasionally, when one of our men was missing, we suspected that he might have deserted. Occasionally, also, a soldier was so desperate to get off the front line that he wounded himself. Doctors could usually tell if the wound was self-inflicted. If it was, the soldier was shot on the spot.

Ivan pushed us back more and more. We fought during the day and retreated at night. It seemed we marched endless distances.

As a messenger, I covered extra miles. As soon as it was safe for me to leave my foxhole after nightfall, I walked back to find out where our next position would be. Most of the men left the front line by ten or eleven. So as to not alert Ivan of our withdrawing, a rear guard stayed on the front line shooting throughout the night. If 2:00 A.M. was the agreed-upon time, I had to be back by then to lead the rear guard to our new position.

In the dark, if the terrain was hilly or forested, orientation was more difficult. Sometimes the rear guard got nervous and left before I was back. Trying to find them brought me sometimes right up to the Russian line. If I heard Ivan talking, I turned around as quickly and silently as possible. Then I had to hunt down the wandering rear guard that weren't really sure where they were headed in the endless expanse of Russia.

One officer, our company leader, had observed me as a messenger for some months. When he was in charge of the rear guard, they always waited for me. One such night, I left at nightfall to find out our position farther west. My way led through forested hillsides to a river. At the river, I went some distance south looking for a bridge. Then I turned north and finally found one. On the other side of the bridge, I heard voices too soft to identify from that distance. I crossed the bridge and approached cautiously to get close enough to hear if they were friend or foe. Hearing German, I called out, *"Schiesst nicht!* [Don't shoot!]"

I identified myself, my unit, and my orders and asked directions to their command bunker.

"Which way did you come?" a comrade asked.

"Over the bridge," I answered.

The three comrades looked at each other. One set a map in front of me. Another held a hurricane lamp so I could see. "Show us which way you came."

I showed them my route, ending with crossing the bridge.

They looked at each other again. "Well, you are lucky!" one said. "The bridge is already mined!"

A lump formed in my throat. I swallowed. I doubted luck was what saved me. I couldn't help thinking of the scripture I'd learned years before and that Mutti quoted often in her letters: "The angel of the Lord encampeth round about them that fear him, and delivereth them" (Psalm 34:7).

"May I look at the map again?" I asked.

"Certainly," they responded.

I tried to visualize the section of the map that showed the territory I'd be walking back over with its forest and hills. It had been the hardest route of any trek I'd led.

On the journey back, I went through the river—better a wet uniform than tempting fate.

I hurried to get back near the planned time to meet the rear guard, making a mental note of the twists and turns of the difficult route. The rear guard was happy to see me. They fired a few final shots, and we withdrew.

Another officer was also with the rear guard that night. When I turned left a short way into the forest, he said, "That is not the way!"

The company leader looked at him and then me.

"I went this way during the day," the other officer insisted, "and I *know* it is wrong!"

The company leader paused. "Grellmann," he finally asked, "which way must we go?"

I pointed. "Left, sir."

He waited an instant. "Lead on, Grellmann."

The other officer fumed.

At the next juncture, the officer was certain we had to go left.

"Grellmann," the company leader asked again, "which way must we go?"

"Right, sir."

"Lead on, Grellmann."

"It's wrong," the officer insisted. "We'll run into the Russian line."

The company leader responded, "We'll follow you, Grellmann."

At nearly every turn, the officer was so insistent I was wrong that I began questioning myself. With the forest and the hills, it was hard to be sure. *God, please give me wisdom,* I prayed silently. *Don't let me lead these men into danger.*

CHAPTER 17

Why Me?
1943

As we walked down one hillside, fog began to settle in, hiding landmarks I was depending on. I mentally questioned if we should turn right in a particular spot or keep going straight. *God,* I prayed, *which way should we go?*

In my mind, I saw us turning right and sensed a peace about it. When I took a right the dissenting officer exploded. "He is heading us into disaster! We have to go straight here!"

"Grellmann," the company leader asked, "are you sure?"

"*Ja,* sir," I said.

"We will follow you," he responded.

Over and over I prayed for wisdom. Over and over, the officer was certain my directions were wrong. Over and over the company leader chose to follow me. It was a frightening compliment—the lives of these men hung in the rightness or wrongness of my decisions.

Finally, we came to the river. We headed north—against the officer's objections. This time I truly felt certain. What a relief when we reached our destination!

Thank You, God! I prayed silently. *Thank You for leading all these men to safety.*

We German troops clearly had lost our initiative. Our division was in nearly constant retreat. Everyone was exhausted—fighting during the day, retreating at night, moving farther and farther west.

One day another soldier and I received orders to find out how far Ivan had followed us. We headed east—on alert. It was a beautiful, sunny day. If I had been home, it would have been a wonderful day for a walk with Hanne.

We came into a village and saw no sign of life. The two of us separated and walked down different streets to see if we could find anyone. The streets were empty. Coming to a collective farm surrounded by a high wall, I heard conversation. I pulled myself up the wall to look over. About twenty civilians were talking with a dozen Russian soldiers, who all carried machine pistols. One of the soldiers saw me. Conversation stopped. All eyes looked at me. I gulped. Their machine pistols looked like the kind that were excellent weapons. They could fire fifty bullets before having to reload or change the magazine.

I looked at the Russian soldiers, and they looked at me. Then the soldiers and the civilians all took off running in different directions.

I dropped onto the dirt street. I could hardly keep from laughing. Here I was, all alone. Or was I really alone?

On Christmas Eve 1943, I met up with a soldier who had received about all the medals a soldier could get. He was older than I and had survived from the start of the Russian campaign. As we visited, Ivan started getting noisy on their line. "They've been given vodka," he said matter-of-factly.

I nodded. "They'll attack to spoil our Christmas."

"*Ja,*" he responded. "And we'll return the favor for their New Year."

The rowdiness on the Russian line increased. "Grellmann," he said before he left, "let's see which of us will survive the longest."

The attack came later that night. That comrade was among those killed.

A few weeks of quiet followed at our section of the front line. I looked at Hanne's photograph at every opportunity and dreamed of the future we would have.

Then, for days we heard the rumbling of tanks and other equipment. Ivan was moving into position. No reinforcements arrived for our line. Of the full complement of 120 soldiers, our company had about 90 men left. The companies around us were short also.

One morning all hell broke loose. We were under heavy bombardment. I was thrown to and fro in my foxhole. I could hardly breathe. Every second it seemed another grenade exploded and big chunks of soil were thrown at me. I was about to pass out. I felt totally defenseless. *God*, I prayed, *please help!*

The attack seemed to last hours, but it was probably only half an hour. When the smoke cleared, swarms of Ivan closed in on us.

We survivors opened fire. The Russian advance slowed.

Ivan broke into our lines on both our flanks, forcing us to fall back. By the end of the day, 36 soldiers were left in our company.

The companies that had given way on both our flanks had their next home leave stopped. My scheduled home leave was two weeks away. *What good is home leave anyway*, I wondered, *if you don't survive until your turn to go?*

The next morning we received the support of two pieces of mounted artillery and were ordered to retake our position from the day before. We succeeded. By nightfall, 15 of our company were left.

Fresh troops took our position, and we were ordered behind the lines. An officer from our division, who had been briefed about the bombardment and how we had stopped the advancing Ivan, praised us for retaking our position and told us we could sleep the rest of the night in a deserted village next to the front.

Exhausted, the 15 of us walked to the village and looked for some protection for the night. We found a cellar with a dead Ivan in it. A couple of comrades carried the body out.

Ober Lieutenant Mahnke said, "We will split up into two groups. Wagoner," he addressed the first class sergeant, "you can stay here with one group. I will take the others."

"*Ja*, sir," Wagoner said. "I would like Grellmann with me."

"No," Lieutenant Mahnke responded. "Grellmann will come with me."

Lieutenant Mahnke and the seven of us with him found another cellar nearby. Finally, we were able to lie down about midnight. I awakened about five the next morning and lay there, aware of artillery blasts, appreciating the privilege of lying down, hearing my comrades' heavy breathing of sleep, and dreaming about the day when I would hear no more of Ivan's artillery.

Suddenly, a grenade hit. The explosion was close. *Are our comrades in the other cellar safe?* I wondered. I slipped out and went to check.

A big hole gaped open where the cellar had been. I looked around to make sure. I was certain that was the place. There was no entrance door. If anyone under the rubble had survived the direct hit, they would suffocate.

I ran back to our cellar. "Mahnke!" I shouted. "Everyone! Wake up! The other cellar took a direct hit. We have to dig them out!"

The men scrambled outside, and we started digging.

Within about forty minutes dawn lightened the area, and Ivan spotted us. They already had the right measure of range and let us have some more grenades. Three more comrades were badly wounded. Throughout our digging, we had heard no knocks, had seen no indication that anyone could have survived.

"Stop digging," Mahnke ordered. "It is time to go. Only 5 of us are left."

As the 5 of us started to leave, Mahnke looked back at the crater. Quietly he said, "So I did it right last night . . . insisting Grellmann stay with me!"

I heard his comment and I wondered.

Mutti's last letter came to my mind. She had closed by saying, "Remember, Georg. We pray for you every day. Here are some verses from Psalm 91 that I claim for you often: 'I will say of the Lord, He is my refuge and my fortress: my God; in him will I trust. . . . A thousand shall fall at thy side, and ten thousand at thy right hand; but it shall not come nigh thee.' "

Did You indeed protect me? I asked God silently. *Why me, when all these others are dying? Why do my comrades seem to sense I am protected?*

Pain and Pleasure
1944

Three years in hell. Two and a half years since I'd been back on the Russian front after being wounded. I hadn't seen Hanne. I hadn't seen my family. I was scheduled for home leave in two weeks. I knew it could be canceled for little or no obvious reason. I was almost afraid to hope it would really happen.

God, I prayed one evening when it seemed I couldn't stand war for another minute, *would You help me survive till I can get home and see Hanne and my family one more time?*

On a beautiful spring evening two weeks later, I climbed aboard a train headed for home. As others elbowed their way to the front of the platform, I willed the train to load quickly, to depart this wilderness before anything else could happen.

Finally, we started to move. As the train gathered speed, a shout welled up from the soldiers. "*Ja!* We're going home!"

Emotion toyed with my mind—disbelief, relief, wonder, delight, thrill, dread. The mood in the car changed to jubilation. No one slept much that first night. I tried to forget the battlefield, yet its images filled my mind. I was excited to be leaving the killing, thrilled to be heading home. Grateful to God who'd protected me. Dreading to fulfill the vow I'd made after Gerhard was killed.

My seatmate was a young man named Rolf. We got acquainted and shared our dreams. Standing on the platform when we changed trains in Przemysl, back to trains for the narrower gauge tracks, Rolf suggested, "Since we're due to report back here the same day, and get our orders, we ought to wait for each other here."

"*Ja,* let's do!" I agreed. We'd enjoyed our trip together. Though I wasn't interested in going back, I might as well have a seatmate I could enjoy.

While at the train station at Przemysl, a comrade standing near me asked a military policeman, "How much behind us is the next train?"

"No more trains," he responded.

My head snapped toward him. Nearby comrades strained to hear.

"General Schoerner canceled all leaves," the military policeman continued.

The comrade's voice rose. "But soldiers were loading on the next train," he insisted. "I was the last one to load on this train. My friend was just behind me."

"They unloaded and went back to their assignments," the policeman pronounced. "This train had just left when the order came through. This one was the last to leave."

I was dumbfounded. *God,* I prayed, *thank You for getting me on a train that's going through.*

I got off the train in Breslau on Friday afternoon. It felt strange not to be going to my old home. But since my parents had moved west to the state of Saxony, seeing them wouldn't come till the next week. I could hardly wait to see Hanne. But I needed to make one other visit first. If I left it till later, I'd only dread it all the more.

I looked up Gerhard's address. At the home, a woman answered the door. She looked my uniform up and down. "Frau Geilke?" I asked.

"Ye-e-s-s-s?"

"I'm Georg Grellmann. I've been on the front lines in Russia. I had the privilege of meeting your son in boot camp, and I got to visit with him the night before he died. I just wanted to—"

"You knew Gerhard?" she questioned, tears welling up in her eyes.

"*Ja,* madam."

"Come in. Come in!" She motioned me eagerly toward the living room. "Tell me all about him."

It was hard to see her grief stricken. I didn't know what to say. How could I tell the truth without saying so much that it would hurt her even more? I wondered, *Did I do the right thing by coming?*

After our visit, when I stood to leave, Frau Geilke took my hand. "Thank you for coming," she assured me. "You don't know what good you've done my grieving heart today. Thank you for caring enough about my Gerhard to come to comfort his mother! Thank you so-o-o much!"

As painful as it was, I was glad I had gone. And thankful Gerhard's mother was in some way comforted.

As soon as that painful visit was done, I hurried to Hanne's apartment. About to burst with anticipation, I rang the doorbell.

Hanne's mother answered the door. Her face brightened. "Hanne," she called, "you have company."

Hanne rounded the corner. Her eyes lighted up. "Georg!" she squealed. She ran into my arms.

I welcomed the Sabbath with Hanne and her parents. Hanne and I had the whole weekend to spend together!

"How is it at the front?" she asked early on.

I closed my eyes. "Sweetheart, I am here. I don't want to even think about war. I am with you. May we just enjoy the time we have?"

Her eyes danced. "*Ja, ja.*"

Our dreams for our future grew as we shared them together.

I stayed the night with Hanne's family. In the morning I downed my uniform and accompanied Hanne and her parents to church. The stained-glass windows, the organ music from the balcony, the smiles of familiar faces all welcomed me. Standing near the front of the church, I saw Rudi's wife come through the door, carrying their baby. Our eyes locked, her face blanched, and she burst into tears.

Rudi must have died in Russia, I thought.

He had. So had Herbert and Fred.

Why am I alive? I wondered. *Why did they die and not me? Especially Rudi, with his new baby.* I felt guilty for still being alive.

The next morning I took the train on to Saxony and looked up my parents' address. They lived in a different house in a different town than before, but it was still home—the same parents, the same furniture, the same taste of potato soup. And hot meals in real dishes. It didn't seem right, though, for Hannchen to be away at Hirschberg for teacher's training and Jo to be away in the army—he'd just headed for North Africa.

Was it two weeks off that I had? Was it three? I don't remember. But I do know it flew by in no time! And it was hard to leave the comforts of home, knowing I was headed back to a series of foxholes in Russia.

On the way through Breslau, as planned, I saw Hanne again. We continued planning our future and pledged again to be true to each other. When I dared not wait a minute longer, she sent with me a parcel she had prepared.

On the train, I felt more discouraged than I ever had. Even the parcel full of *kuchen,* candies, and other goodies didn't lift my spirits—though I did decide I'd make them last as long as I could. At Przemysl I went to the front car of the train as Rolf and I had agreed. He wasn't there. I found a seat, set my parcel down next to me, and turned around to look for him.

As I peered toward the back of the train car, I sensed trouble. I turned around. There was no parcel on the seat beside me. There was a parcel in the hands of a soldier walking forward in the car. I went after him and tore the parcel out of his hands.

What a mean thing to do! I spluttered to myself. Anger rose in me. Rolf never showed up, and I had no idea what had happened to him.

I didn't know a soul and was not interested in getting to know anyone. I hated the thought of heading back to where life was worth nothing. But orders were orders.

That night we slept on bunk beds with sacks filled with straw for mattresses. Lying on my bunk, I opened Hanne's package and ate— peppermint, *kuchen*, chocolate. If I saved any, I might never get to enjoy them. I was alive at that moment. Who knew? Maybe it was my turn to get gunned down during the first two weeks back in the trenches and foxholes.

I had so looked forward to going home. But I hadn't given a thought to going back to hell's front line. And I couldn't bear to think about it now. I ate until there wasn't a crumb of Hanne's gift left that could be stolen or that someone else would eat after my demise.

Chapter 19

Why?
1944

I didn't know a soul in the new company. Even though I survived the first two weeks back on the front line, I felt sorry for myself. At least we'd been in one spot long enough to join some of our foxholes into trenches.

"Been on this front for long?" the comrade next to me asked quietly.

"Got back from home leave three weeks ago," I said. "Other than that and two months off to heal after a mine got my leg, I've been on the Russian front forever. Lot of time in the Ukraine. My company was headed for Stalingrad when I was wounded."

"Oh-h-h," he groaned. "Stalingrad." He took a couple deep breaths. "I was wounded there. They flew me out just before Germany lost two hundred and fifty thousand men there." He shuddered then his voice brightened. "You're back fighting. Your wound must not have been too bad."

"No," I answered. "Just took some cleaning up and healing."

"You were one of the lucky ones," he assured me. "Getting wounded was the only way to get out of the Stalingrad theater. Given the way they treated their own men, I'd sure hate to be Ivan's POW."

"What do you mean?" I asked.

"Well," he said, "when I was there, there was still a bridge standing over the Volga River. I was near it. Our weapons and machine guns had control over the bridge. It was suicide trying to cross it, but the Communist commissars drove the poor Russian soldiers across to their deaths. If they tried to turn back, their own men shot them.

"And we'd run out of food," he continued. "About to starve and still forced to fight."

I heard a noise off to the east and moved down the trench. Nothing came of the noise, but I had plenty to occupy my mind. Being wounded and the trip to get help had been awful. But from everything I'd heard, my company had made it to Stalingrad. Had I not been wounded, I would have been there too.

Here on the withdrawing front line in the Ukraine, I lived one minute to the next. The summer sun was almost unbearable. Shade was nonexistent. Water was often hard to come by.

At one point, the no-man's-land between Ivan and us was a field with ripe tomatoes. One scorching day we had nothing to drink and no way to get anything. The ripe tomatoes grew more tempting as the day wore on. But no one was interested in doing the harvesting.

By midafternoon I almost could taste sweet, luscious tomatoes. But the thought did nothing to soothe my cotton mouth. So, I started figuring, *If I crawl flat along the ground, I should be OK. The bullets fly too high to get me down there.*

A comrade came up with a basket. I snaked toward the tomatoes and started picking as fast as I could.

My basket was half full when Ivan's grenade throwers went into action. The grenades landed to my left.

It'll take a couple minutes to get them better targeted, I thought.

I picked all the faster. Filling the basket and pushing it ahead of me, I made it back to the trench before Ivan got me targeted correctly.

My comrades hadn't had any interest in picking tomatoes, but they were happy to share in the harvest I gathered!

The war dragged on. We'd hold a line for a while and then withdraw again. Days turned into weeks. Summer heat turned to chill autumn. We withdrew through harvested fields.

One day I was headed on an errand. Because I was out of reach of Ivan's light fire, I walked upright. I heard several grenade throwers shoot. It's almost impossible to tell where they are aimed. The grenades go high into the sky and then come down like a bomb. When you hear one coming down, it's too late to do anything.

One came down right at me. Instinctively, I dove face-first. The grenade exploded before I hit the ground. It turned me in midair so that I landed on my back. I closed my eyes while the dust settled. I realized I could still feel my arms. They moved. I could still feel my legs. My feet and legs moved also. I rolled and sat up. Everything worked fine.

This isn't good luck! I realized. "God," I whispered, "I don't know why You saved me, but thank You."

Days later, on another errand, I walked through a field and was out of range for Ivan's light weapons. This time he shot off artillery grenades. These I heard hurtling through the air, coming my way. I hit the ground, my feet toward the oncoming explosion. One hit the ground fifteen feet from me. It didn't explode. It skidded along the ground, still not exploding, and stopped at the soles of my boots. Unbelieving, I looked at the grenade. Explosions had erupted on either side of me. One grenade didn't explode—and it came to rest at my boots.

Again I wondered, *Why, God?*

At one point when the lines stabilized, I was ordered behind the lines to a training unit. After brief instruction, I was promoted to corporal. I wasn't sure I wanted the promotion. Before, though we worked as a unit, I was ultimately responsible only for myself. As a corporal, I was responsible for others—maybe ten, maybe fifteen, depending how many men we had lost and how many had been replaced.

The fallen were replaced by newcomers. They were on our team, but I knew nothing of their skills. One night I went along our positions from foxhole to foxhole—we no longer had time to dig connecting trenches. One newcomer was asleep. I took his gun and then woke him. He came up fighting.

"Comrade, Corporal Grellmann here," I said, desperately trying to be loud enough for him to hear, but quiet enough not to attract the enemy. "I'm German."

He fought me with one hand while reaching for his gun, his shovel, or anything he could get his other hand on.

"Comrade, calm down," I whispered huskily, avoiding his fist. "Comrade! I'm German! Corporal Grellmann."

His arms stilled. *"Kapo?"* he questioned, using the common battle-front slang for corporal.

"Ja."

His shoulders relaxed. He sighed.

"You were sleeping," I whispered. "You put your comrades at risk."

As dark as it was, I could see the whites of his eyes grow larger.

"I'll not report you tonight," I added, "if you *promise* me you'll never sleep again when you're supposed to be awake!"

"Ja, Kapo! For sure!"

I handed his gun back to him.

As the weeks passed, this comrade hung around me when he could. One afternoon, he seemed agitated. With distress he started, "Oh-h-h, *Kapo* . . ." Then he sighed.

"Ja?"

He just stood there shaking, terror filling his eyes.

"What is it?" I asked.

He shook his head. "No, no," he moaned.

Several times later, the same comrade started again, desperately,

"Oh-h-h, *Kapo* . . ." But the conversation went no further. I urged, but he wouldn't continue.

Whatever he was thinking troubled him greatly. I wondered what he knew that was too heavy to carry alone and yet too terrifying to share.

The front lines stabilized for a while.

"I haven't gotten any mail for forever!" I overheard one soldier complain to another corporal. "We're stabilized again. You'd think the German Army could get a few letters through to its heroes!"

"I don't know when we'll get any," the corporal replied. "But I'd sure like some too!"

Shortly, sections of the front line again withdrew westward as the rain and cold of late autumn came. Earlier, Ivan were at times poorly dressed and equipped. But things had changed. Now Ivan had more tanks than we, more artillery, more planes in the air. And he seemed to have an inexhaustible supply of men.

After a couple of weeks of heavy fighting, the whole front line began to move again. The division's headquarters withdrew first, then the regiments and artillery. We in the infantry went last.

Sometimes while we withdrew, we were cut off from the rest of our troops and surrounded by Ivan for days or weeks. During daylight we dug in and defended ourselves. During the night we fought our way along, moving west. Rations got smaller and smaller until we received one slice of bread and two cigarettes per day. A smoker and I exchanged commodities—my two cigarettes for his slice of bread.

After a few days with no sleep and nights of marching, exhaustion overtook us. Soldiers who could no longer move were left behind to fall into the hands of Ivan. At one point I was so exhausted I couldn't lift my arms, but my legs moved . . . one step at a time . . . though I was half asleep.

At one place while we withdrew, we went through a railroad yard. The railroad cars had been set on fire to prevent Ivan from using them.

Passing by, I glanced at the cars. I couldn't believe my eyes! They were filled with letters and parcels. Car after car of mail—burning.

The troops around me marched on, rushing to stay ahead of the enemy. I stopped and stared, dumbfounded, beside the railroad car of burning mail. *Why wasn't it distributed?* I wanted to scream at some officer who had been safely at the back of the lines making decisions for soldiers who were dying on the front line.

Ivan was right on our heels. One of my comrades missed me. He turned and yelled, "*Kapo,* come on!"

I hardly cared. In my rage, I purposelessly turned over parcels that hadn't yet burned. *A letter would have given us hope,* my mind raged on. *Could have encouraged us. Could have given some of those men who gave up the will to survive. Could have comforted those who didn't. We've had plenty of times when the lines were stable—they could have brought us mail! These cars have been here for days!* I fumed. *And hearing from home is like dreaming of heaven.*

"*Kapo!*" several comrades screamed. "They're almost there! Come on!"

CHAPTER 20

Training
1944

Rage burned within me. If I didn't move quickly, there would be no escape. I rolled over one more package.

My mouth dropped open. I blinked and looked again. The parcel was addressed to me . . . in Hanne's handwriting.

A chill ran down my spine. Suddenly energized, I grabbed the parcel and ran.

That night, snow fell hard. Our line crossed a harvested sunflower field. I gathered dried sunflower stems and covered half my foxhole. The sunflower stem roof kept the snow off, but my feet still got cold, and I got cramps in my legs. I opened the parcel from Hanne—candy, cookies, and *kuchen* that was nearly dried up. I ate and thought of my sweetheart and was glad she was safe and not suffering. She was not accustomed to deprivation. Her father had a government job, and their family lived in upscale housing. Being an only child, she could have, it seemed, pretty much anything she really wanted. *I hope I will be able to provide for her, as well,* I thought.

Thinking of Hanne was such a contrast to the moment's reality. On the front line, we lived like animals and worse at times. No hygiene, no toilets, no brushing of teeth. We wore the same underwear for months. As the fields got soaked from rain and dried again, so did we. In times of frost, ice, and snow, our slice of bread was frozen. By this time, I was the only one in my company who still carried a backpack. Still, we fought, we retreated, we tried just to survive.

Between Christmas 1943 and 1944 the front line withdrew steadily westward—Zaporozhe, Dnepropetrovsk on the Dnieper River, Nikopol, Odessa, the rivers Bug and Dniester. Heavy battles were fought in Moldavia—Ivan lost more than two hundred tanks. The front line stabilized for some time along the River Prut, near Iasi, Romania.

One day I got a new order—report to a training unit near Iasi. Most of the men there had been instructors. Some had been stationed in occupied countries or in the homeland for years, their positions considered essential for the war effort. Up to now, all had been spared fighting on the front lines. But Germany was a small country. She was running out of young men to fight. These soldiers had been combed out of their cozy jobs to head for the front line.

My new assignment was to train these professional soldiers how to adapt to the war in Russia. Among twelve of us instructors, I was the youngest. The powers-that-be gave me the soldiers who were highest in rank and were also the oldest. They all far outranked me. Most were old enough to be my father. And they knew all the tricks of the trade. They were unhappy about leaving their old jobs, unhappy about being there, and most unhappy about where they were headed. They were unhappy about the humiliation of taking orders from a kid.

I wasn't much happier about my job than they were about theirs. It wasn't my thing to shout orders. My only qualification for the job was that I'd survived on the Russian front for three years.

As much as I hated the job, I thoroughly enjoyed being out of the trenches. The army billeted me with a peasant family near the school. I ate at the training unit but slept in their home—warm and comfortable. What luxury—a small room to myself, a real bed, and I could keep myself clean!

Stately mulberry trees, essential for silkworms for the silk industry, lined the road on which I walked back and forth to town. They hung full of beautiful and tasty white, yellow, and purple fruit. I didn't have to watch behind every tree for guns or artillery trained on me.

One day I found a cherry tree, full of inviting fruit glistening in the sun. All the other trees had been harvested. I picked a cherry, popped it into my mouth, and . . . puckered up. It was sour! But no more sour than the soldiers I had to train. And the cherry had something I could enjoy—flavor.

I took off my backpack and got out my metal bowl and mosquito net. Picking cherries till I had quite a pile in the mosquito net, I then twisted it tighter and tighter, squeezing the fruit till the bowl filled with cherry juice. Refreshing!

After about a week, my students and I got along well. They sensed that I didn't relish giving orders, but we all knew orders were orders. I followed those I was given. They followed those they were given.

Soon the sour cherry tree was about picked clean, and I'd enjoyed every drop of the juice. I also discovered plums and enjoyed the abundant fruit, whatever the variety. The locals made wine from much of the fruit.

The training sessions each lasted three weeks. When one was done, I got another group of men old enough to be my father and with ranks well above mine. We had a tough first week again, and again settled in.

The much-higher-ranked commanding officer in charge of the training school had a double doctor's degree and had taught in the University of Breslau. Somehow he discovered that I liked to play chess and invited me to join him one evening. We played till early morning, and we had many more all-nighters after that. Sometimes he won, sometimes I did. We both enjoyed the challenge. I learned to respect him highly. Whether playing chess or leading the school, he was very thoughtful, balanced, and prudent.

Being in the military in a foreign country wasn't popular or easy. But mail got through—both directions. The letters from Mutti and Hanne encouraged me, but loneliness dogged me often. When the other instructors went to town on the weekend, I joined them. Some got happy after a few drinks and some got mean. I remembered my early vow and drank water while they drank their wine. Before long they badgered me. "Aw, come on, Grellmann. A little wine never hurt anyone." "Grellmann, you like fruit. A little wine made from good, wholesome fruit won't hurt you."

I ordered plum wine. I enjoyed the flavor. Next I tried cherry wine. Then plum again. I didn't see that I was acting foolishly. My cohorts congratulated me.

About midnight we left and walked toward the school. I stumbled over a tiny stone but caught myself so I didn't fall. Then, for no reason, my step lurched to the left.

Immediately I knew the small stone on the road wasn't the problem. It was the stone in my head that had been too hard to hear and heed the promptings of the Holy Spirit. Anger flared up. *You failed!* my mind pummeled me. *You're no Daniel who stood true even when faced with death! You caved in when you just faced a little pressure! How would you like Hanne to see you now?*

"No!" I gasped.

How would you like Mutti to see you now?

"No!"

I remembered one of the bedtime stories Mutti had read to Hannchen, Jo, and me many years before. Herr Schmidt was good to his wife and children . . . as long as he was sober. But when payday came, he spent all his wages at the beer joint then went home and mistreated his family. Of course, then, they had no money to buy food and to pay bills. Herr Schmidt's habit had started innocently—"I just had a few social drinks," he told his wife. But soon he was hopelessly enslaved.

Late one night at the beer joint, another customer pointed to Herr Schmidt and asked the owner, "Why don't you send that drunk home and close up?"

The owner glanced at Herr Schmidt and grinned. He must have thought Herr Schmidt was too drunk to hear because he said, "I give him all the drinks he wants until the kernel of his soul is gone. His wife can keep his shell."

But Herr Schmidt heard. He left the beer joint, the words repeating themselves in his mind. On the way home he thought about his wife. She had been a beautiful young woman, and the beer joint owner had asked her to marry him. She had declined. Instead, she had married him—Herr Schmidt.

The beer joint owner's words rang in Herr Schmidt's mind again— *"I give him all the drinks he wants until the kernel of his soul is gone. His wife can keep his shell." He's getting revenge by giving me alcohol,* Herr Schmidt realized. *My wife is still a beautiful woman. The only thing that makes her less beautiful are the worry lines I have given her. I have hurt my wife. I have hurt my children.*

Herr Schmidt stopped and looked up. "God," he said, "with Your help, I will not touch another drop of alcohol!"

By the grace of God, Herr Schmidt never drank again.

I didn't want my mistakes to hurt Hanne and the children we planned to have. I didn't want to fail God again. I looked up, beyond the stars. "By the grace of God," I said, "I'll not touch another drop!"

The next Saturday night I went with the instructors again. I drank water. When I no longer drank with the guys, their attitude toward me began to change. It seemed I was no longer a friend but a silent voice badgering their consciences.

One night two instructors got mad at each other and pulled out their pistols and started shooting at each other. As long as they were drunk enough to get crazy, it was a good thing they were drunk enough not to aim well. After that, if some men got drunk, the sergeant major and I would collect their pistols.

After three or four weeks, the officer in charge of the training unit, the sergeant major, and I were dispatched to a Romanian army base for two weeks to demonstrate some of our latest weapons, especially the bazooka. The Romanian soldiers stood in formation before every meal and prayed. The officers, down to the rank of corporal, ate separately. They didn't pray. We were invited to join the officers. There we were served like in a restaurant. Some spoke German. There was much light talk and much laughing. You would have thought there was no war going on. Judging by their questions, they were more interested in German drugs to control venereal disease than in war and weapons.

Observing the contrast between the common soldiers and the officers, I recognized that discipline in the military is based on rank and not on the value of a person. You may dislike or disagree with an officer all you want, but, because of his rank, you have to obey him. On the front line I hadn't seen the overbearing attitude. You were all working together to save your hide and that of your comrades. You soon learned whom you could truly respect and whom you couldn't.

Back at our training school, we heard that the Romanian oil fields had been bombed. There was cautious discussion about how much the Romanian government could be trusted and what the different possibilities were—if they changed sides, the German divisions and trainers would be surrounded and lost.

One night several of us were standing outside looking up at the stars. Just to make conversation, I remarked, "And some people believe our fate is determined or influenced by them and their positions."

"Grellmann," our commanding officer barked, "how can you say such a thing? I would not have expected that from you!"

I didn't expect a reaction like that from him either. It was so unlike him. I shut up and just wondered what was going on.

Is it just the general edginess? I wondered. We all sensed something was brewing. Politically, it felt like the quiet before a storm. Foreboding rested heavily on our minds. The temptation to get drunk and forget our troubles was strong. On Sunday night we walked into town to the restaurant again. They gave us a room by ourselves.

The instructors ordered a round of drinks—my order was for water. As they drank, they got more foolish. When one man yawned, one of the servers said, "Whoever gets tired ought to pay for the next round."

"Ja, ja," they agreed. "This round is yours."

Pitcher after pitcher disappeared, but none would admit he'd had enough. Some even began pouring their drinks under the table but still wouldn't admit to being through. I picked up from the two young women who served us that they wanted to get all the money they could from us tonight so they could get fabric for new dresses the next day. I became increasingly annoyed with the instructors and the servers. Finally, when the servers left to fill the pitchers again, I followed them down into the cellar. I knew what I was risking. So be it. "If you fill those pitchers one more time," I threatened, "I'll lock you in this cellar."

They laughed and reached for wine bottles.

"I'm not joking," I said. Disgust poured from my voice.

They took the pitchers back to the table . . . empty. I stood outside the room, listening.

"Why didn't you bring more wine?" the instructors drawled.

"Because this young corporal threatened to lock us in the cellar if we brought any more," one said.

"Ja," the other corroborated.

There was an instant of icy silence. I thought it best to enter the room.

The staff sergeant cleared his throat. "Grellmann," he shouted. "Who do you think you are?"

The party was over.

Next morning, duty began as early as usual. I was fine. The other instructors were out on the drilling field, nursing their headaches. Before long, the coldness made it clear I was no longer welcome among the instructors. I sensed they'd like to rid the school of my presence. To get rid of an instructor, you could either help them get promoted or demoted. I felt certain none of them would be recommending me for a promotion. I sighed. *Looks like I'll see trenches again.*

Escape
1944

I had just one hope of staying out of the trenches—our commanding officer (CO) appreciated me. The disgruntled instructors would have to come up with a plausible reason if they wanted to get me demoted.

Everything was quiet for a few days. What was happening behind the scenes? I didn't know. Then I received orders to go for special training to Doeberitz, not far from Berlin.

At supper, the commanding officer asked me to come to his office when I finished eating. There he asked, "Will you be stopping in Breslau to see your fiancée?" he asked.

"I'd surely like to!" I said.

"With all the interruptions in travel," he said, "no one will question you about how long the train trip took if you stop for only one or two nights."

My heart started racing. *I'll get to see Hanne!*

"As you know, my parents live in Breslau," the CO continued. "Would you mind delivering a letter to them while you're there?"

"Not at all," I assured him. "Be glad to."

He handed me his letter. "Best wishes to you, Grellmann."

I walked into town. The train left Iasi about eight o'clock that evening. When we reached Vienna, Austria, the next morning, I got off the train to stretch and get some fresh air.

Instead, my breath was nearly taken away by the news. Overnight, Romania had defected from Germany and, at the same time, allowed Russian motorized divisions to move through their front line to the south and north of German army units, surrounding them. The train I was on was the last one out!

The news sent chills up and down my spine. My latest company was most likely among those surrounded. *What about the German instructors at the training school?* I wondered. *And the CO? Are they dead? Were they taken prisoner?*

I was safe in Austria. I climbed back on the train, headed for home soil.

My heart was heavy for all those I knew in Romania. Yet, I was thrilled to be safe. *God,* I prayed, *I don't know what You have in mind for me, but whatever it is, help me do it.*

As the clacking of metal wheels on rails speeded up, I realized something else. I hadn't been very tactful in the way I'd last handled the issue of alcohol. In spite of that, God had probably used my bungling efforts at standing up for principle to send me here to safety.

I wondered about the future of my country. If the German government went under, what would be the consequences this time? Would more people starve? And what about my own future? I had been promised a scholarship . . . by the German government. If the government failed, there would be no scholarship.

A young German soldier from the same division joined me on the train. His uniform sported the *Ritterkreuz*. He was small, quiet, and unassuming. He hardly seemed a candidate for the highest German medal given for bravery.

After visiting awhile I asked, "How did you get the *Ritterkreuz?*"

"Did you say you were from Breslau?" he asked.

"Ja," I responded. He clearly wasn't interested in talking about his medal. I dropped the subject.

We talked of home, of sweethearts, of dreams. Eventually, battles came up. He told of situations where it was amazing that he had made it out. I told him of the grenade that landed at my boots. Of mines that hadn't exploded. Of a mine that had saved my life—had I not been wounded by it, I likely would have died with 250,000 others at Stalingrad. I told him about my friend's wife bursting into tears when she saw me alive. "How do you deal with it?" I asked. "Sometimes I feel guilty for being alive."

He nodded. "Boy, do I understand that," he said. "One day I accidentally dropped into a Russian trench. Either they would get me, or I would get them." He shuddered. "Panic stricken, I fought down the trench. Eighteen died." He motioned toward his shoulder. "Army gave me the *Ritterkreuz* for that." He closed his eyes and took several deep breaths. "I would rather cry than celebrate." He swallowed hard. "War is horrible!"

"*Ja!*" I agreed.

"How do you handle what you saw?"

We had the same questions. We didn't have answers.

I got off the train at Breslau and found the home of my commanding officer's parents. His father was a general in the upper echelons of running the *Reichsarbeitsdienst*—the youth work camps. Their section of town and their apartment made it clear they belonged to the leading class of society. When I proffered their son's letter, they invited me in. "Tell us all about him," they insisted. "Is he well? Is he happy?"

I told them about the great evenings we'd spent together playing chess. I told them of his thoughtful, prudent handling of affairs, of the respect I had for him and that most everyone at the school had for him.

They were pleased. Then his mother said, "I worry about him. I shouldn't ever think about it," she said, "but I can't help it. Before the war, a group of the city's leaders hired a man who wrote horoscopes to be the entertainment for a New Year's Eve party. He wrote out a horoscope for every person there. My son read his and showed it to me. 'If I ever need to look for a job,' he said, 'I can use this for a résumé.' It described him that well. But there was one horrible part," she continued. "It ended by saying one day he would be responsible for his own death . . ."

Suddenly I understood why the usually calm CO had shouted at me for my comment about the stars.

His mother wiped her eyes with a handkerchief and then went on, "I haven't had a peaceful night of sleep since then. Especially after he went off to war. And now . . ." She wiped her eyes again. "Now that the Russians have surrounded the German troops in Romania—"

Her husband jumped in. "Have you heard anything since then?"

"No," I said. "He was the last one to see me off at the school. That's when he gave me this letter for you. Later that night the Romanians defected. My train was the last one out."

The CO's mother wept quietly. His father wrung his hands. "I know what they say on the front line," he said. " 'Save your last bullet for yourself.' And he's an officer. For him to become a POW would be even more demeaning."

"I'm so afraid," his mother said. "So afraid he'll take his own life rather than fall into the hands of the enemy." She sobbed and then added, "I would go into hell for him if only I could help him."

Later, walking to Hanne's apartment, I thought about their words. A simple thing like a horoscope. But, oh, what pain it had caused! For him. For his parents.

I thought of the palm reader in the Ukraine. I was glad I didn't even listen to her predictions.

The words of a scripture hit me. "The thief cometh not, but for to steal, and to kill, and to destroy: I am come that they might have life, and that they might have it more abundantly" (John 10:10).

The devil's out to steal, kill, and destroy, I thought. *He sure took the sunshine out of their lives with that horoscope. And he's doing a thorough job of killing and destroying with this war. Wherever we use his methods, life is devalued. God wants us to live life to the full.*

The visit with Hanne would have seemed "life to the full" if only it didn't have to end! Two nights there—a bit more time to dream and plan. Then I had to go on.

The train trip from Breslau to Berlin took only a few hours, and I reported to the big military base and training grounds at Doeberitz, just outside Berlin.

Again, I felt like a stranger. I was among officers. One sergeant and I, a lowly corporal, were the only noncommissioned officers. Each of us was given command over a company, and we practiced war games, some with live ammunition. Six weeks later, as we were finishing training, one

At the end of 1944, Georg as a corporal on a short visit to Hanne after he had left Romania, on his way to Berlin

evening I felt hot. I felt my forehead and headed for the medic station. They sent me by train to the army hospital in Berlin. My head ached, and fever burned in me. I didn't just think I might die, I wished I would.

By then the city was suffering frequent air raids. The allies had landed on Normandy and were retaking France. The outlook was gloomy. I wondered if I would die from the malaria or if a bomb would take me out first.

Within days I was pronounced well and ordered to go to the division from which I had come. One problem—that division no longer existed. The army couldn't be bothered with such details. They sent me south via train. In Vienna, I was given new orders—return to the home base of my division in Alsace-Lorraine. I set out to retrace my train trip and then go a little farther west.

By then, many German cities were under heavy bombardment. All the communications and services were disrupted. Bombs hit the train ahead of us. We helped those who were alive and then walked on, getting to another train after several hours. We arrived in Wuerzburg just after an air raid. The city was on fire, and rubble filled the streets. The rail line had been bombed, so my train couldn't make it through. I was under orders and had to make it to the other side of the city.

There wasn't just a fire here or there. Everywhere I looked, flames filled the windows or leaped into the sky. Smoke billowed above the city, made visible by the light of the fires. Sirens pierced the night air, punctuated by various screams and wails. I tramped through the rubble toward the River Main, which flowed through the city.

If it's like this in Wuerzburg, I wondered, *what's it like in Breslau? In the towns of Saxony? Is Hanne alive? Are my parents?*

The river was the only open way through the city. I walked along the bank. I couldn't grasp the disaster before me, behind me, beside me.

My Own Country
1945

I had grieved because of battlefields littered with bodies. Even the deaths of Russians brought me no pleasure. I mourned at cabbage fields decimated, sunflower fields flattened, farmland mined. The destruction of whole cities was more than I could wrap my mind around.

The river quietly lapped at the bank, but there was no peace.

The next day I found another train on the west side of the city and made it as far as the River Rhine. There our train was bombed in broad daylight. Passengers rushed off the train and threw themselves into the ditch next to the railroad line.

When the planes were gone, since the train was disabled, I walked on.

On the way to the next village, an American plane appeared. We called them Jumbos. In front they had machine guns, but they could also drop bombs. I was the only one on the highway, so I paid them little attention. They wouldn't bother with one man.

Or would they? The plane flew over me and then turned back. It descended and flew right above the highway. I hit the ditch. The machine guns went into action. The bullets hit all around me. I lay motionless till the plane was long gone. I would be more careful in the future, even if I was alone.

About midnight I traipsed through Bingen. On the cobblestone street, the metal on my boot heels announced every step. Suddenly, a bullet whizzed by me.

The bullet must have come from a basement window on the other side of the street. It was impossible to know which one. It would have been foolish to investigate. I moved on quickly. *Has it come to this?* I pondered. *Being shot at in my own country?*

Finally, I got back to my base camp in Alsace-Lorraine. They kept us exercising and going through routine maneuvers until new units could be organized. After duty hours and on weekends, we could leave the camp. A comrade invited me to go with him to visit friends. Since I had no other plans, I agreed.

I thought we were going to visit family friends, but the greeting from the young woman wasn't that of a relative. That night my comrade joined her in her bedroom.

She tried to persuade us to stay. "I'll give you civilian clothes," she promised, "and hide you till the war ends."

I only knew to obey orders. Besides, I was under oath. And I had a fiancée. At 4:00 A.M. we got up and jogged back to camp to make it in time for roll call.

Near the end of the week, the same comrade invited me to go with him again.

"How could you do that?" I asked. "You are married and have a child. No, thank you! I am not interested to go with you again to that house!"

Sunday afternoon I was surprised to see him on base. Monday morning he came to see me. "I stayed here this weekend," he said. "I knew if you would not go with me that I should not go either." He held out a telegram he had just received from the neighbor of the woman we had visited the week before. "Direct hit Monday 1:00 A.M. All lost."

Had we gone as he had planned, we would have been among the dead.

I received orders to report to Idar-Oberstein again. There I met a comrade who had been wounded three times. Knowing the war was grinding to an end, we questioned if we had any options.

One evening he took me along to a home where he knew the people. I was surprised how openly they discussed the end of the war. One elderly man said, "When the allied troops come, I will go out to meet them with a white flag. I will welcome them." Neighbors dropped in. One man played an accordion, and others had other instruments. They played and sang as if they were already celebrating the end of fighting.

Hoping the war would end soon, my friend and I decided on a plan to gain time. We volunteered to become officers.

A week later we received orders to report at Wiesbaden for officer's training. On the way, we saw smoke ahead. The city of Mainz had been bombed during the night and was burning. Military police ordered everyone in uniform to help people save some of their belongings. Rushing to stay ahead of the fires, we carried furniture from apartments and loaded it onto every kind of available conveyance. But, for a city, there was precious little furniture that hadn't already been demolished by the bombs or burned in the fires.

Smoke filled the air. People were crying. As well as cursing the enemy, they cursed Hitler and the government. "Where are the miracle weapons the government promised?" people screamed.

I felt numb.

When I arrived at Wiesbaden, classes began. Our class had been there only a week when we heard the rumble of artillery coming from the west. Two more days and we had orders to assemble. "American troops have established a bridgehead east of the River Rhine," we were told. "The Fuehrer ordered that you, along with the *Volkssturm*, must push them back."

The *Volkssturm* was made up of men too old for the military but who could still carry a gun, and fifteen- to seventeen-year-olds from the Hitler Youth. We at the officer's training course were to lead them. Everything was done in haste. We didn't know each other, had never trained together, and were ill-equipped. All together, we made one company—about 120. We had no back-up.

I was given a group of fifteen. Some had weapons. Others had none—including me. Still, we marched off according to orders. On the outskirts of town we passed a house with a pretty flower garden in a fenced yard. A woman stood in the door of the house. "Madam," I called, "could you give me a spade?"

"*Ja,*" she said. She went around the corner of the house and came back with a spade with a long handle.

"Thank you," I said. I'd learned in Russia the importance of being able to dig in.

We arrived at the ordered position after dark. My assessment of the situation was that the Americans had crossed the River Rhine without meeting any resistance and had occupied several villages. They protected themselves through the night with an umbrella of continuous artillery and mortar fire around the places they now occupied. Besides ground troops, they had tanks and heavy weapons. Shooting all the time told us they weren't short of ammunition. In my estimation, we'd be totally unable to do them any harm in daylight. Our only chance was trying to attack during the night.

In the darkness, we found our way into the middle of the bridgehead and waited for the order to attack. Heavy fog began to settle on the field. Hour after hour passed, and no order came. I told my group that if we waited for daylight, we would be in a mousetrap between the occupied villages and would have no chance. The longer we waited, the more my suspicion grew. Had those who gave us orders left to seek their own safety?

My gut feeling was to withdraw in the same direction from which we had come. I told the group my decision. Some were ready to follow, some undecided.

If I get out of this, I decided, *I'm going home.*

I just started to leave when the others called me back. "An order came," they said "to withdraw, by going that way." They pointed in a direction that set my teeth on edge.

It seemed crazy, but I'd followed orders all the years of the war. Against my own judgment, I followed orders again.

Dawn was just starting to take the edge off darkness. We got only a short way when we must have become visible to the Americans. Machine-gun fire pinned us down.

In the increasing light, I started digging with my spade. I'd gotten only about twelve inches deep when bullets barely missed me. I flattened myself to the ground. Whenever I moved a little, bullets whizzed by again. With one arm I reached a dead comrade and pulled his body in front of me. Then I could turn in my shallow hole without being seen.

The sun rose. We were in a potato field that had been harvested. Heaps of potato vines lay all over the field. Before long we also received artillery and mortar fire. Unlike the Russian grenades, the American ammunition caused a lot of smoke. Each time a grenade exploded, I ran from one heap of potato vines to another.

That went on for quite a while.

I got about halfway to a small forest. If I could get to it, I was sure I could stay hidden through the day. By daylight tomorrow I'd be miles away.

Again I thought, *If I get out of this, the war is over for me. I'm going home.* Just thinking such a thing surprised me. I'd obeyed orders every moment for more than three years. But I felt betrayed. I had fought for fairness. I had fought for the reunification of German peoples. I had fought for the safety of an idealistic society that would treat all people equitably. Something awful had happened. Why had we killed hundreds of thousands of Russians in a land far beyond our lines? Why was Germany in shambles?

I heard the rumble of a plane approach and then fly low over the potato field. It began to circle around me.

Moments later, soldiers swarmed toward me. "Surrender!" they shouted. "Surrender and you won't be hurt!"

I had no weapon.

I had no choice.

I stood and lifted my arms in surrender.

CHAPTER 23

Prisoner
1945

The American soldiers led me to the others of our company who had survived—about sixty or seventy. The boys of the Hitler Youth hugged me. "Oh, *Kapo*," they exclaimed. "You're alive!" They laughed and hugged each other. "We're alive!" they rejoiced. "We're alive!"

The older men and I didn't share their jubilation. To become a prisoner of war was not honorable. We had failed our country. We had failed ourselves. We had lost our freedom.

The American soldiers lined us up and went through our pockets. They took everything, including the small picture of Hanne, the last letter from her, my watch, my small Bible, and my address book. They didn't take the small gold band that was my engagement ring. And they didn't find my pocketknife, which I had gotten into the habit of keeping in my boot.

That done, we were ordered to our knees with our arms stretched forward.

After a while, some arms started to sag.

"Arms up!" a soldier barked. "Keep them up!" He lifted a couple of arms with the barrel of his rifle.

Eventually, some men could endure no longer and fell over.

In my mind I knew it was just the military way of teaching us who was boss. It was meant to help us obey for fear that something worse would happen.

While we were there, lines of American soldiers began marching by—seemingly endless numbers. Trucks, jeeps, tanks, and heavy equipment moved forward without interruption. There were already thousands of soldiers east of the Rhine.

My sense of betrayal grew. The leaders of the German military must have had some idea of the resources that waited at the Rhine. It was ridiculous to send one thrown-together, untrained, ill-equipped company to fight them. What kind of cruel joke was that?

About noon we started marching. We reached the Rhine in late afternoon. Many small boats ferried troops from the west bank and then took some of us on their return trip. Observing the levity and lack of skill of the boatmen, I guessed some had been in the wine cellars. Several boats capsized. Steering through the POWs, other soldiers came to the rescue of the crew. Propellers cut some of the POWs. Some made it to shore. Some drowned.

We were herded into a makeshift camp in an open field with barbed-wire fencing surrounding us. For food, soldiers distributed canned army rations. My pocketknife was much in demand for opening cans. I had carried that knife since I left home, and it had become an all-purpose tool. Others' knives had broken, but mine just kept on cutting fingernails, bread, cans, and anything else that needed a knife. I could easily sharpen it on a stone and keep right on using it.

Several days passed, and then we were loaded onto trucks and driven through Cologne and Aachen. Both cities had been badly bombed. Few people were in the streets. Mainly, just women dressed in black. Was all of Germany mourning? I had the strange sense that it was the end of civilization.

In Holland, we were put on a train that headed southwest. It passed through Paris. When civilians recognized us as German prisoners of war, many drew their hands across their throats as if to say someone ought to cut our throats. Children showed their disgust even more than the adults. We got off the train at Cherbourg and were marched across the city. Children threw stones at us. Some women spit at us. It was almost a relief to get to the holding camp near the harbor.

There we wondered about our situation: *We are prisoners of the United States. We are in France. England is just across the English Channel. What will happen to us?*

In one respect, being a POW was similar to my time on the Russian front—we knew nothing of what was going on in the world around us, knew nothing of the future of our own little world, knew only what was happening at the moment. And so we waited.

The day came when we embarked on a ship in the harbor—a small, six thousand–ton ship of the Liberty class. None of us were allowed to go on deck. Some near a porthole saw the coastline of England. As they lost sight of the English coast and the ship continued due west, it became clear we were being sent to America.

Quite a mix of men was on board. The oldest was seventy; many were young. Quite a few came from Austria and other countries, but the homes of most were in Germany. Some were laborers, some had learned a skill, others had obtained a good education. A few lost the respect of the majority by bragging about their sexual exploits. Most spoke of their families with longing—whether sweethearts, parents, or children.

When we reached the high sea, we were allowed on deck for an hour each day. The salt air was a great relief from our crowded quarters below. While on deck on May 8, 1945, a guard told us the war was over—Germany had surrendered.

A rush of feelings came over me and hounded me. A thrill that the horror had halted. Wondering how Hanne was, how Mutti and Vater were, how Jo and Hannchen were. Questioning if they were alive. Sadness at my own position—I'd survived the horror of the Russian front line only to lose my freedom within days of the end of the war. Instead of heading for Hanne and home, I was headed to God-only-knew-where for God-only-knew-how-long.

Germany had lost. Its government would probably fall—if it hadn't already—and even if it didn't, the economy would probably be so bad that they wouldn't honor nonessentials . . . like scholarships. I would be on my own for building a future for myself.

But at least I am alive, I pondered. *And God* does *know where I am and where I'm headed.*

I hadn't really given God a lot of thought during the war. I thanked Him once in a while when His protection was so clear that the soldiers around me saw it. I kept morally pure. I avoided alcohol, except for the one time. I kept my oath to follow my country's orders. I rarely thought about Sabbath—most of the time on the front line I didn't have a clue what day it was.

But even though I had failed Him, God had kept protecting me—even when I didn't know it. Like the leg wound—if it hadn't been for that, I likely would have been lost at Stalingrad. Like leaving the Ukraine for home leave on the last train that got out. Like getting transferred out of Romania and leaving on the last train out. Like living through the train bombings. Time after time of protection on the battlefield flashed through my mind. God had been watching out for me.

Conviction came over me that I needed to do what I knew was right. *God,* I promised, *as soon as I am free to do so, I will keep the Sabbath.*

As the days wore on, men began to dream of their future. Some of my bunkmates began making plans to band together and open a business in the United States. "Grellmann, you're good with numbers. You can be our accountant."

My plans had gone down the drain—my scholarship wasn't worth the paper the certificate was printed on. Some of their plans sounded interesting. But they weren't Sabbath keepers. I made up my mind. I would not get into a partnership in which I wasn't free to totally obey God.

When I hesitated, one sneered, "Grellmann thinks he's better than us."

That was far from the truth. But they wouldn't understand if I tried to explain.

We disembarked in New York Harbor. A husky guard had learned to say "Hurry up" in broken German. *"Machen sie schnell!"* he shouted at me and then kicked me on the backside. He laughed a hearty belly laugh.

If I sped up I would run over the guy in front of me. I looked straight ahead, keeping my place in line.

We were "processed" there—stripped, showered, and registered. I lost my precious knife there. Then we were led to a train station and climbed aboard a passenger train. "Wow!" the man behind me exclaimed. "This sure beats the cattle car that carried me in Russia."

"*Ja.* And the freight cars," I added.

We rode day and night. We had to get permission to stand or go to the toilet. Soldier's provisions were delivered at meal time. In the morning the man ahead of me looked out the window. "We're still in America," he said to no one in particular.

"*Ja,*" his seatmate said. "And still passing forests and fields and industrial plants." Motioning out the window, he added, "Think of their resources."

The first man shook his head. "And our government gambled our lives against all this."

The second afternoon, we came to a camp. Old-timers there said we were south of Okalahoma City. The food wasn't bad. The average German had never heard of peanut butter. We called it monkey fat and called jam Truman marmalade. The bread was made from fine flour, like cake, and had little substance. We had a library and an orchestra. We could play soccer, tennis, and other sports, and we gave theater performances. We could see movies.

These things were fine, but it was a bit of information that gave me hope, that helped me hang on to sanity in the midst of uncertainty. A man taken captive in the North Africa campaign said he had learned that governments had agreed in Geneva Conventions about how POWs were to be treated. The part that interested me most was that prisoners of war were to be returned to their home countries within six months after the war had ended. I did some quick calculation. I didn't know exactly what day the war had ended, but the guard on ship told us about it on May 8. So, even by the worst case scenario, I would be headed home by November 8.

I smiled. *Sure, I'd rather be home now. But after three years on the Russian front, I can take most anything for six months.*

A big tortoise plodded around camp. Somebody who had time enough on his hands to think up mischief had painted a red swastika on its shell. None of the guards seemed worried about it.

Our armpits were checked several times. I couldn't figure out why until someone explained, "The SS have tattoos in their armpits."

Civilian examiners came into camp and interviewed each POW individually. "What did you think about the war?" "What can you tell me about the Nazi party?" "What do you think of Hitler?" Besides asking questions, they watched every move I made.

I didn't know what it would lead to, but I had to be honest. On one hand, I had to admit Germany had committed wrongs—at times on the front line even I had felt betrayed. On the other hand, I had grown up with patriotism. I believed there was more right than wrong about my country. I loved my homeland.

We interviewees discovered we were classified into three categories: One, those supportive of Hitler and his government. Two, those who could prove they had been against Hitler. Three, the gray area—those who were more or less noncommittal.

Some of the older men who had belonged to political parties against Hitler before he came to power had a chance to convince the examiner that they were against Hitler all along. Some of them were repatriated. As far as we could tell, they were very few and far between.

The examiner assigned me to the "gray" category—undecided. At the time, that was true.

One night we were required to see a specific movie. It showed soldiers with German uniforms. Jewish people wearing armbands with yellow stars arrived in cattle cars and were herded into buildings surrounded by barbed-wire fences. The narrator spoke in German of those who had been in the camps for some time, and the film showed men in some places, women in others—all were skin and bones. It showed gas chambers. The narrator said that Hitler's Germany had exterminated millions of Jews for no reason other than that they were Jews. He said that people who hid Jews got the same treatment.

I shut it out of my mind. I couldn't absorb anymore. It couldn't be true! It couldn't be!

Imagination?
1945

None of us could believe the stories about the holocaust. It became the subject of much discussion.

"It's true Hitler didn't like Jews, but he never would have done that!" one said.

"No," added another. "Look at all the good he did for Germany. Like the youth work camps—a main emphasis was the equality of *all* people."

"I sure didn't fight for that!" one of the veterans of the Russian front exclaimed.

"Me either," a whole group of us chorused.

"I didn't always agree with Hitler," another said, "but he wasn't heinous. He might not have liked the Jews, but he would never be so cruel as to starve civilians or gas them and burn their bodies."

"The Allies won the war," concluded another, "and they're just trying to come up with some moral justification. This holocaust thing . . . it's just somebody's imagination. It *couldn't* have happened!"

About once a month we were given air-grams to write letters home. I hoped I remembered my parents' new address. I wrote in small letters so I could say as much as possible. "Are you safe?" I wrote. "Is

Hanne safe? Is she still at the same address? Please send me her address if she's moved."

I wanted to ask about the Jews. But the Americans had told us their story. We were supposed to believe what they said. I figured our letters would be censored, and I didn't want anything to keep my letter from letting my family know I was safe or to keep me from hearing back from them.

Then we waited for return letters.

More required movies were shown—more "holocaust imagination," as some called it. One night, a man not far from me jumped up as the film rolled. "That was me. That was in an air raid in Mainz." He stood, silent for an instant. "See! That is where I lived."

The film rolled on. Before our eyes, our comrade's apartment house took a bomb and exploded.

We were somber after that movie. At least some of what they were showing us was real.

As soon as we were given the opportunity to work, I volunteered. I was sent by train night and day across more vast lands to Arizona. I had never seen country like it—no house, no tree, nothing but sand and hills of sand. We perspired greatly and were given salt tablets to eat. Then we were off to a big camp in California. That camp had a dental station, and I applied to work there.

The next thing I knew, someone reported I was a Nazi. "You were blackmailed," a comrade told me. "Two dental technicians are already working at the dental station. They started the rumor because they were afraid one of them might lose their position."

The evidence supported my comrade's claim. *Das Vorurteil*, I thought. Mutti's comments years ago about prejudice had come to mind from time to time through the years. It hit me again. Prejudice is not just about differences. It's about meanness in a person's heart.

I didn't have a chance to answer the accusation—I was in the next group being transferred. We came to a smaller camp of tents near Stockton, California.

Finally, I got to work. At first I helped load fifty-five-gallon barrels of gasoline onto railroad cars. Then I pressed khaki trousers and shirts in a laundry at night. Hot! During that time I was supposed to sleep days—in a tent under the summer sun. Scorching! For a night's work I received eighty cents in coupons that I could spend at the canteen.

The German leader at that camp was a dentist, and some of the helpers in his office came from Silesia where I had lived. It was fortunate I'd gotten acquainted with them. One day they came looking for me. "We need a medic. Are you interested in the job?"

"Ja! Ja!"

I got a tent of my own, worked days, and could sleep at night when it was cooler.

One of the required films said that the men of Breslau did not believe it when the Allied troops said the war had ended. They fought on for three days. My heart moaned. *Beautiful Breslau. Where is Hanne? Is she alive?*

The months passed. At each opportunity, month after month, I wrote a letter home. I begged to hear back and printed clearly the return address we were given. I pleaded for information about Hanne. No replies came.

Sometimes at night I lay in my tent wondering, *Did all of Germany perish before the war ended? Am I truly as alone as I feel?* I fingered my ring and pictured Hanne's eyes. I dreamed our dreams again and wondered, *Is she alive?*

And what of my family? At least Jo was in the army. Is he alive someplace else like me?

I received no mail. But then, all the other POWs talked about not receiving mail either. Surely not everyone in Germany was dead. The fact that no one else got mail either gave me an inkling of hope.

POWs in the U.S., at Stockton, California. Georg, working as a medical orderly (top middle) and two office workers

I began counting the days till November. Any day now, we should hear when we'd leave for home.

November rolled around. November 8 came . . . and went.

Would I ever get out of this POW camp? Would I ever get to try to find Hanne and my family?

It so happened that two chess masters lived in this camp—one from Vienna, one from Cologne. To pass the time, I jumped into the competition. I played my first game on a Sunday with the man from Cologne. The game lasted through the night, and he lost. Both of them loved to play with me since I didn't brag when I won. For me, playing kept my mind off my worries and my frustration.

During the day I kept an eye on the health of the camp. At least once a week, I held inspection. If anyone was really sick, I took him to see a doctor.

Once I went with a patient to San Francisco. The doctor came into the examining room and turned to me. "Why did Hitler kill the Jews?" he asked. "Yet, here you bring a patient, and we treat him."

By then, I had grasped enough English to get the drift of what he said. But I didn't speak English. And what could I have said? If it was real, I had no idea why he did it! It certainly was not what I fought for!

I couldn't help wondering, *Could it be true? Could Hitler have ordered millions of Jews exterminated?*

I thought of the Germany of my youth—a beautiful country. But there was unrest between different groups—Germans and Poles, Catholics and Protestants, Communists and Nazis, Jews and Gentiles.

I remembered the morning of the liquor smell in the dental lab and the discussions that followed. Even then, some had rumored it was Hitler's elite guard who had damaged Jewish businesses. Could it have been?

Kristallnacht. *Was the night of broken glass just the beginning of years of broken dreams?*

At the POW camp, one of the mandatory movies said that soldiers who would not willingly participate in the concentration camps were sent, instead, to fight on the Russian front. I remembered the officers who, for punishment, had ended up fighting next to my company in Russia. It was plausible that others, too, could have been punished with a similar assignment.

Suddenly, a new thought startled me. I saw in my mind's eye the young comrade whose gun I had taken when he had gone to sleep. I heard the pain in his voice, saw the desperate expression on his face when he said, "Oh-h-h, *Kapo* . . ." *Had he been asked to work in places like the films showed? If he had, no wonder he was horrified.*

One day a guard showed a group of POWs some photographs he'd taken when he was in Germany with the U.S. Army. Each scene of the German countryside made me homesick. I longed to smell the scent of fresh-mown hay, to feel the crunch beneath my feet as I hiked the familiar hillsides for pleasure, to hear the evening sounds as the sun set in my homeland as my family was seeing it—if they were alive. Why hadn't I gotten an answer to any of my letters?

My mind came back to the moment. The guard pulled another photo off the stack in his hand. His face broke into a grin. He handed out photos of several nude young women and bragged about his exploits with these German Fräuleins.

I walked away. His attitude disgusted me. The German soldiers I knew had believed in protecting our country and the defenseless women and children. We were willing, if need be, to give our lives to protect the decency of our citizens. It was obvious, even in a glance, that the Fräuleins in those photos were not struggling to get away. Even if they cooperated for food, they gave away their decency.

The Fräuleins in the photos struck another blow to my diminishing patriotism.

Then I remembered a German soldier after the campaign in France bragging about what he had done with French girls and the few German POWs on the ship coming to America who bragged about their exploits. It struck a blow to my diminishing respect for humankind. Was any side any better than the other?

Letters
1946

The months passed—seven, eight, nine. I received no mail. Neither did anyone else. Some POWs tried escaping to Mexico. Heat and thirst forced them back. Two men approached me about joining with them in an escape to Canada.

I listened. They were a thoughtful pair who had good ideas themselves and were open to hearing my input. We developed a plan. We dried bread. We saved peanut butter. We fine-tuned the strategy. One managed to get a fishhook, line, and weights. We hid supplies in my medic tent. We hadn't set a date but felt we would have everything ready within days.

When I got up that night to walk to the washroom, extra guards walked the fence around our camp. For whatever reason, all 250 of us were moved to another camp.

Shortly, we were told we had been "good boys" and all of us would be sent home. It sounded good. But if they were really sending us home to Germany, why did they strip us of other clothes and give us all new uniforms—black with large white letters on our pant legs, shirt sleeves, and the backs of our shirts. The white letters announced clearly, "POW."

We were put on a train, and it headed east across the vast country.

We spent about ten days in a camp on the East Coast. "You will be going," they promised. The few items we intended to take home with us had to be spread out on the ground for inspection. Then we boarded a ship.

For some, it was the death of the dream of staying in America. For others, it was a long overdue return home.

All the questions of the past months played over and over again in my mind. What had happened to my parents, my sister and brother, my fiancée? Were they still alive? Why had none of us received any mail? Could we really trust that we were being sent home? Ever since I had donned the army uniform in my homeland, uncertainty about the future was my constant companion. I was eager to part company with it!

Then stories began to circulate on the ship—we would be sent to France or England but not home. The rumors indicated that even though fighting had ended, the Allies said they were not obligated to return POWs until a peace treaty was signed. It seemed a discouraging reinterpretation of the Geneva Conventions. So much for parting company with uncertainty.

About the tenth night, the ship anchored in a harbor. We saw many lights. Where were we?

We began to disembark. English soldiers met us and marched us into a camp. We'd arrived at Liverpool, England.

Snow covered the ground. Rain began to fall. Fifteen men were assigned to each four-man tent. We received nothing to eat or drink.

We were cold, wet, and hungry. There was no place to get warm, no place to dry out, and no food or drink. In the tent, our legs inter-twined with each other's as we tried to get all fifteen men in horizontal position. "This is probably better than if we'd landed in France and been put to work in their mines," one optimistic soul offered from the middle of the huddle.

By and large, we were too depressed to appreciate his optimism.

Once the British army got us organized, we were distributed to various POW camps. My destination was Lincolnshire. Not one of us sent there knew another.

Again we were given opportunity to write a letter. Again I wrote home. Would I hear anything this time?

Right away, we were put to work in the community surrounding Lincolnshire. First I was put in a group working on farms picking potatoes or harvesting flax and other crops. Then I searched for unexploded land mines on the coast. I felled trees and cut and chopped wood for fire-wood. Then I worked at a sewage treatment plant.

POWs in Lincolnshire, England. Georg—middle in the front row. POWs on the left still have black POW uniforms; those on the right have been allowed to wear civilian clothes.

We missed the California weather. The housing and food were less desirable too. But the biggest difference was in the atmosphere. War had come closer to the British. The Americans had experienced no air raids on their cities. Here, when we worked in the community in our POW uniforms, we were often treated rudely and with contempt.

But *one* thing was definitely better. When I came back from work one day, the officer in charge had a letter for me! It looked like Mutti's handwriting. But wasn't it shakier than it ever had been before?

I tore the letter open.

Dear Georg,

We were so happy to hear you are alive. We have not known for a year and a half what happened to you and are so happy to hear you are alive and in England.

Hannchen is here with Vater and me in Saxony. Hanne and her mother were here for a while. When the front line came close to Breslau, a number of the church members fled here. They slept on the floor. Finding food and preparing it for everyone was hard. But we all survived. All the guests are gone now.

Hanne and her mother insisted on going back to Breslau. They didn't know that the province had become part of Poland. We are glad we gave them blankets and clothing. When they arrived, they discovered their apartment house was destroyed. They looked for friends and finally found some. Together they cleared a damaged apartment and moved in. But then a Polish family claimed it for themselves. That happened several times. But now they have moved to West Germany.

Mutti gave me Hanne's address. She closed her letter by saying, "Jo is in a POW camp in Scotland. In his last letter, he sounded discouraged. You ought to see if you could get a transfer to his camp."

"*Ja!*" I nearly shouted. "They're alive!"

"Family?" a guard asked with uncharacteristic gentleness.

I blinked. "Oh, *ja. Ja.* My family and my fiancée."

The guard smiled. I smiled back.

I lost no time getting a letter off to Hanne assuring her of my continued love and recounting the dreams that could maybe come true in the near future. I also wrote another letter to my folks. Even work went better—every day when I got back to the prison camp I checked first for mail.

I also took Mutti's suggestion and requested a transfer to the camp in Scotland where my brother was. I was disappointed when my request was denied, but nothing could dampen my anticipation of a letter from Hanne.

One evening it was there! I tore off to my room to savor every word.

She first told about getting back to Breslau, as my mother had written, and about how hard it was to find food and to stay alive. She continued,

As Mother and I were walking in the street one day, a man seemed to follow us. He called to us, and we became afraid and walked faster. But it seemed he called our names. We stopped. As he came nearer, we heard clearly it was our names he called. It must be somebody who knew us, but we didn't recognize him.

Then he stepped up close. "Marta, Hanne. It's me, Rolf."

We looked in amazement. It was hard to believe it could be Vater. It didn't look like him. He was so skinny, so weak. He looked so tired and old. But it was Vater. It was so good to see him.

He went through so much in the war in Breslau, then a POW—he nearly starved to death.

A professor I knew at the University of Breslau before the war got so bad had befriended a Polish professor before the war. Now the Polish professor is in charge of the University of Breslau. Through the good offices of those two professors, they obtained permission for my family to get on a train that left for West Germany. Food is easier to get here. Vater is gaining a little strength and is beginning to have life in his eyes again.

I have found a place to study at the University of Goettingen. I room with another student. Her brother sometimes visits and has begun to show me his attentions.

I am studying basic courses.

I am glad you are safe and well.

Hanne's letter shocked me. She was my fiancée. She was a warm and bubbly person. The letters I treasured through the war were full of dreams and love. This letter was so . . . so noncommittal. Why would she even say that someone else was showing her attention? I wrote her again and awaited her reply. Each day I rushed back from the farm on which I worked and checked for mail. Finally, it came. I tore open the envelope—a photograph fell out. I picked it up and looked at it. It wasn't Hanne. The face didn't have her eyes. I looked at the letter.

Dear Georg,

It is good you are safe and well.

I am sorry to tell you that my roommate's brother is persistent in courting me. I cannot resist him longer. It isn't so much a matter of love but of feeling responsible for my parents. I am an only child, as you know, and my parents lost everything in the war and are now destitute. My friend is a doctor and will be able to help them.

I am enclosing a photo of my best girlfriend, along with her address. She is interested to hear from you.

Dreams
1946

I wandered toward my barrack but walked past it. I felt numb—as though I was in a glass ball that someone had shaken till the make-believe snow swirled around. I was vaguely aware of a world outside, but I did not see it . . . or hear it . . . or feel it.

Eventually, I recognized a vague sense of hunger. Immediately nausea overtook me.

Darkness had come by the time I wandered back to my barracks. I went to bed but only wet the pillow with my tears. I got up again. The moon mocked me. I walked to the fence and grabbed hold of a wire between barbs. *Here I am, totally defenseless, behind barbed wire.* I thought. *I can't go see her. I can't do anything.*

The forest beyond the border beckoned me. I climbed over the barbed-wire fence. If a guard saw me and shot me, I didn't care. I walked into the forest. Up a hill, down the other side. Tears streamed down my cheeks.

"What do you mean, he is persistent?" I asked aloud. "Did you not bother to mention you were engaged?"

My boots beat the harder on the forest floor. I came to a lake that sparkled in the moonlight.

Did her mother encourage her to marry a doctor who could provide for all of them? Who am I in comparison? Just a POW. Maybe I'll always be a POW. Is she just more realistic than I?

In my mind, Hanne's face surfaced again. I saw her as clearly as I had hundreds of nights on the front line when I looked up to the moon and dreamed. But this was no dream. It was more like a nightmare. I wanted to wake up, but I couldn't.

I could almost hear her words from our last visit. "Soon we will be married." "I will be waiting for you." "My heart is yours forever."

Forever.

Hanne's letter played itself over and over—*sorry to tell you . . . persistent . . . cannot resist him longer . . . responsible for my parents.*

I had trusted her. I had kept myself for her and her only. When I was too exhausted to take another step, I had kept picking up one foot at a time for her. When I could not stand one more minute of being a prisoner of war, I had kept slogging for the joy of holding her in my arms, for the dream of forever together.

I fingered the gold band on my finger. There would be no together.

". . . sorry to tell you . . ."

My heart sobbed, but there were no tears left.

I pulled my engagement ring off and flung it as far as I could over the lake. The tiny "splat" echoed in my brain. I felt my life sinking slowly to the bottom of an ocean. No matter what happened, up till now, our dreams had always held me. Hanne had been my reason to live.

I collapsed onto a log, staring toward the lake, seeing nothing.

An owl hooted from the forest.

"*Never* trust a woman with your heart!" I spat the words.

Women will steal your heart and rip it into shreds.

The tears came again.

And what good are dreams? Hitler gave me a gold medal. Ja. He gave me a dream. Then he stole back the future he promised me.

Minutes ticked by between outbursts of thought.

And politics is no answer. Certainly not Hitler. He started out great. But look at the mess he got us into! Giving lousy orders that got hundreds of thousands killed on the battlefield. Killing Jews by the millions. Why didn't somebody stop him? Where were all the German politicians?

The horrors of the images of the holocaust haunted me. The cries of dying soldiers on the battlefield tore at my mind.

Communism certainly isn't the answer. I knew that when I was a kid seeing the demonstrations. Stalin didn't improve my impression any!

And the United States. Holding POWs beyond when they agreed to themselves. And England's doing it too.

Disillusionment grew.

All the European governments. Grubbing for land and power. Stealing property. Not caring one whit about people.

I swallowed hard. "Never trust anyone!" I said.

Spent, I finally plodded back to camp. I was almost sorry some guard didn't see me climbing over the fence and get some target practice.

Days dragged by. Nights were worse. I barely ate.

One day on lunch break at the farm I grabbed a chicken, wrung its neck, and stuffed it in a bag. After work, I smuggled the dead chicken back to camp. I didn't have the slightest idea how to pluck the feathers or cook the bird. Another POW helped me with that. We found an empty can in the garbage and set the chicken to cook on the coal stove in the barracks. When I figured it had cooked long enough, I took a spoon to check it.

Another man saw what was happening. "Grellmann," he gasped. "I didn't think you could do such a thing."

Time stopped, frozen.

The thought of eating stolen chicken suddenly turned my stomach.

Shame filled me. I had done what I despised in others. I couldn't even trust myself!

I turned and walked away from the chicken, away from the coal stove, away from the barracks. I walked hard, fast. But I could not march away from myself. I could not escape from conscience.

God, I pleaded in a silent scream, *can You forgive me?* I gazed through the barbed-wire fence into a sullen sky. The air was still. Inside my mind, a storm raged. *Or are You even there? Do You care about us humans? Is life just a cruel joke?*

Other POWs received letters also. Many had lost whole families. Dreams decayed to dust. Hope turned to despair. As the bad news increased, so did suicide in the camp.

As I saw the grief of others whose loved ones had died, I thought of many a fallen comrade. In my mind I saw the shallow graves, the quick burials. I saw the soldiers left lying on the battlefield—some dead, some simply too starved and spent to take one more step. Death would have claimed them soon . . . or worse.

I thought of friends from home—Herbert . . . Fred . . . and Rudi, with a wife and a new baby who needed him. It made no sense.

Why did they die? I cried out to God.

In the face of so much death, I felt guilty for living.

You kept me alive, God. But, why?

I was transferred to a smaller camp near Lincoln. One of the guards at this camp was a proud corporal who would argue with anyone. And he *had* to be right. One evening he asked, "What is German for 'lights out'?" A POW responded, *"Fruehstueck,"* which actually means "breakfast." The guard proudly marched through the camp shouting, *"Fruehstueck, fruehstueck."* The men grinned and turned off the lights.

No-fraternization laws were being eased. Occasionally, when we could get a guard to take us on a Sunday, fifteen or twenty of us would go to church. We couldn't understand much of what was said, but we had a desire for something spiritual. It seemed to take a slight edge off my hopelessness.

Another Christmas approached. In POW camp, holidays just made us miss home and family more. Suicides increased in the camp. Days felt dismal. That year one of the men discovered the *Messiah* would be performed at the local cathedral.

If only I could go!

Every day I wished I could hear the grand anthems of the *Messiah* again. My hurting heart longed for an evening of peace and beauty.

I discovered another man who wanted to hear the concert too. We talked over the situation and recruited help. On the afternoon of the concert, two men who rode bicycles to work hid theirs in some bushes outside the camp. The two of us disguised ourselves as civilians as best we could. After dark, we climbed over the fence, found the bicycles, and rode into town. As the conductor lifted his baton, we slipped into the back row of the cathedral.

Beautiful stained-glass windows lined the sanctuary walls. The orchestra and the choir joined in majestic harmony, the likes of which I'd not heard since before the war at concerts in Century Hall in Breslau. My hungry soul sat at a banquet table. I drank in the sweetness. For one evening, I was a whole man, lost in the beauty, the majesty, and the harmony.

"For unto us a Child is born, unto us a Son is given . . ." The strains lifted me higher and higher. "And His name shall be called Wonderful, Counsellor, the Mighty God, the Everlasting Father, the Prince of Peace."

Ja. *There is a Messiah,* I thought. *A Savior.* Though it seemed like an impossible dream, I prayed silently, *God, could You give me hope this Christmas? And peace?*

For the finale, everyone else stood and joined in singing the "Hallelujah" chorus. I wanted to sing along, but I could pronounce no English words.

After the echo of the last "Al-le-lu-ia" had stilled, the woman on my left quickly took my hand and pressed into it something hard, flat, and round. Then she turned and left.

I was so shocked I just stood there, mouth agape.

My companion poked me. "Let's go," he whispered.

I stepped into the aisle, and we headed for the bicycles. Then I looked into my hand. The woman had given me a coin—a half crown. Our disguise had not fooled her, and she had reached out to me—a symbol of those who had caused her country so much pain. She had reached out to me with a gift. Warmth filled my chest and sent a tingle down my spine.

Hope
1947

That Christmas, the government announced permission for civilians to invite POWs into their homes for a meal. Herr Taylor came to our camp and offered to take four to his home for Christmas dinner. The camp dentist and I went along with two men from the office.

We were taken to one of the little red brick houses sitting close together along the streets. When we entered, it seemed familiar yet strange. Then it hit me—I hadn't been inside a family dwelling since I helped carry furniture out of bombed buildings in Mainz, since before I left Germany, since before I was betrayed into surrender. The table was set with a tablecloth, real porcelain plates and cups, and plenty of delicious food. For years, I had seen only metal army containers used for food. The final contrast was three young women sitting on the other side of the table.

All we POWs were out of touch!

Herr Taylor was in his seventies and had a heart condition. When he felt the need to lie down, he did so, unceremoniously, on the floor beside his chair. Frau Taylor was hard of hearing, and her hearing aids didn't seem to help much. Their daughter, Mavis, had a friend on either side of her. None of them knew German. Only one of us could speak any English. But we enjoyed the food and thrilled at the human warmth.

Dinner with the Taylors felt like an answer to my concert prayer. That Germans and British could sit amiably across a Christmas table felt like a little sample of "Peace on earth."

Yet, from time to time, my war experiences rose before me. One night especially, my sins seemed as tall as the Caucasus Mountains, as ugly as a pile of rotting bodies. *You killed,* a thought taunted.

I was only following orders, I said to myself. Yet, my chest felt a heaviness—the same distressing burden I felt each time a deadly front line memory forced itself into my conscious thought. I tried to bury the thoughts, but they kept rising up. I argued with them, but the guilt did not rest.

No! I wanted to shout. *Don't think about it!* But strains from the recent concert derailed my habit of trying to bury the painful past. The melodies in my mind played through bits and pieces of the music. War memories tried to drag the music into a lower key, but, instead, words started to fit the music. "Every valley shall be exalted . . ." "For unto us a Child is born . . ." "I know that my Redeemer liveth . . ." Just the title of the oratorio was enough to plant a seedling of hope—*Messiah.* There is a Savior.

You played a part in killing, the voice tried to speak over the music in my mind.

Yes, I answered. *I did. And it was horrid.* My conscious admission surprised me. *But,* I hurried to say, *there is a Savior.*

I thought back to the Bible. Moses murdered an Egyptian, but God forgave him and used him. And David. The killing of Uriah was awful too.

"God," I prayed. "What should I do with the ugliness of the past?"

"Give it to Me." I sensed His whisper.

"But it is ugly," I said. "I don't even want to see it myself, let alone show it to a holy God."

"But as long as you try to keep it all buried, you will spend all your energy shoveling denial . . . or good works . . . onto the mountain. I have

something better planned for you—freedom. If you will give all the garbage to Me, I will wash you clean."

First John 1:9, I thought. *"If we confess our sins, he is faithful and just to forgive us our sins, and to cleanse us from all unrighteousness."*

To be forgiven for all the pain I had been a part of through the war seemed too much to ask.

Another text from childhood came to my mind. *"For God so loved the world,"* I quoted, *"that he gave his only begotten Son, that whosoever believeth in Him should not perish, but have everlasting life."* Jesus didn't say "whosoever other than people who did bad things." Just "whosoever."

"No sin is too big for My grace," God seemed to whisper.

"God," I prayed. "It seems too big to ask. But I believe You. Please forgive me."

I didn't know what enemy soldiers I had killed or wounded. Visions of various battles came to mind. "Forgive me for that," I pleaded over and over. Finally, no more war dead rose in my mind. "Forgive me, please," I finished, "for every death, for every bit of pain I caused."

Often Mutti had quoted Psalm 103 in her letters. God seemed to whisper verse 8 into my soul. *"The Lord is merciful and gracious, slow to anger, and plenteous in mercy."*

Gracious. Slow to anger. Plenteous in mercy. The thought thrilled me. *Plenteous in mercy!*

In the quiet, peace washed over me—a peace I had never known before. I felt clean. I felt exhausted but at the same time strangely exhilarated. I wasn't sure if it was angels or my own heart singing the "Hallelujah" chorus.

A dentist who had been in the German Navy worked in this camp in Lincoln. He occupied two adjacent rooms in a large building—one for his dental business and one for sleeping. Each room had a fireplace. When he learned I was a dental technician, I became his assistant—almost his personal servant. I cleaned and sterilized instruments, made models and set up bites and dentures. I looked for scraps of wood and unburned pieces of coal at the city dump to keep the fire going in both fireplaces.

He had a difficult, unhappy disposition. But he had one quality that endeared him to me. He respected a Seventh-day Adventist in his hometown of Oldenburg. With no hassle, he gave me Saturdays off.

About three months after Christmas, no-fraternization laws relaxed more—POWs were permitted to leave the camp on their own on weekends during daylight hours on condition that we wore our black uniforms with the white POW emblazoned on every piece.

Sabbath morning I went to the police station and tried to make them understand I was looking for a Seventh-day Adventist church. They directed me to a place nearby, to an upper floor above a restaurant.

I found the building and climbed the stairs. When I opened the door, all twenty heads turned and looked at me as if I had come from outer space. I found a seat quickly, but I still stood out in POW uniform. They smiled and tried to welcome me, but I couldn't speak English, and no one there spoke German.

The speaker said some words. People turned pages in their hymnals, and music started to play. When I heard the tune, I stood automatically. Everyone else stood, too, and began singing English words. During my years in the army, we always had to stand at attention while the national anthem was played. *But . . . why are the people in this English church standing to sing the* German *national anthem? Are they trying to make me feel comfortable?* I wondered. I wasn't feeling comfortable. I was shocked! Besides the question of enemy nations, I couldn't believe the mixing of secular with spiritual. Watching the proceedings, it took quite a while for the pounding in my temples to quiet.

The folk were friendly enough. After church, the Baldwins invited me to their home for lunch.

From then on, I attended church regularly. I picked up more English words and got to know some wonderful British Christians who took me into their homes and hearts. They didn't just talk about grace—they showed it to me.

Some time after my initial church visit, the German national anthem was played again. Shock hit me again. But this time I recognized some of the words—"Zion," "Rock of Ages," "salvation," "Redeemer," "Jesus." The

Mr. and Mrs. Baldwin in Lincoln, England. Mr. Baldwin was a local church elder. The Baldwins invited Georg home after church the first Sabbath he, as a German POW, attended the local church in England. Georg spent many Sabbaths with them. They were among those who contributed food items for Georg to send to his parents. The Baldwins remained friends with Georg as long as they lived, Georg and his family visiting them in England on several occasions.

tune was the same, but these British Christians sang to that tune a hymn about God, "Glorious Things of Thee Are Spoken."

Attending church and visiting with Christian people gave me something to look forward to from week to week. Yet, I felt torn—enjoying the fellowship but feeling guilty for being *able* to enjoy it. So many had died. *Why me?* I began asking God again. *Why did You keep me alive?*

The questions badgered me for weeks. Slowly, a few pieces of the pain puzzle began to fit together. Jesus Himself, the most undeserving of pain, suffered the depths of evil's worst. Then there was John the Baptist. Surely he and his followers were praying. But even though Jesus said there was no greater human being ever born, John's head was lopped off by a wicked king.

Over time, I realized that whether someone lived or died, if they went through good things or ill on this earth, I didn't know why. I couldn't know why. But the God who looked on me with "plenteous mercy" cared about each one of them just as much as He cared about me. He eagerly waited to have us all together in a pain-free future, to answer *all* the "why" questions. The God I trusted to forgive me, I could also trust with the memory of those who had fallen. I could trust them *and* myself to Him.

The enemy of humanity—the devil—came to steal, kill, and destroy. But Jesus came to give life—abundant life! It was OK to enjoy.

My spirits began to lift. I was alive, though I should have been dead. Each day I awoke was truly a gift from God. "God," I prayed, "help me use each day to Your glory."

I continued to write home and receive responses. In one letter I asked, "Is there anything I can do for you?"

Vater responded. "It is worse than after World War I. If you can send anything, send only items of food."

I read volumes between the lines. After World War I, two hundred thousand people had starved to death in the part of Germany where my parents now lived. People were so poor they felt blessed to be able to give one potato as a Christmas gift . . . and the receiver was grateful! The industries of the area were mining, textile factories, and toy making. But the mountainous terrain and weather allowed very little farming and almost no gardening.

With the little I could save, I began to send food parcels. It felt good to get my attention off myself and do something for someone I loved. I mentioned what I was doing to someone at church and, shortly after, church members sometimes gave me canned food to include in my packages.

As I got to know more people in church, some expressed concern for me being alone. Different ones introduced me to a variety of single young women. I was polite to each but attracted to none. Though I couldn't have her, my heart had been Hanne's for so long that I didn't know how to take it back.

Other POWs didn't feel the same way. One met and married a

British Baptist girl. Once when I was talking with him, I asked, "Hans, isn't it strange for you, believing in Communism, to marry a girl who believes in religion?"

"No problem," he responded. "I'll just keep her occupied . . . with theater, concerts, soccer games, and other entertainment. She'll forget about religion."

Hans could hardly fathom that I believed in the Bible. But he never went so far as to call me stupid—probably because when we played chess, he never won.

Every chance I had, I encouraged his wife to be true to God.

Finally, we at camp got the announcement that all of the POWs would be allowed to go home. Repatriation was scheduled in the order we were taken prisoner. Since my capture was so late in the war, I'd be among the last. I could handle a little longer—as long as it really did come.

My parents were pleased to hear I'd be free, but Vater wrote: "I see no future here for young people." I wrote to a couple of relatives. In both cases, their houses were full—they'd taken in other relatives and were having a hard time feeding those already under their roofs.

When the dentist left for Germany, I was moved with others to a POW camp at Alford, on the east coast. They found various jobs for me, including night watchman at an army vehicle park. But our main work was going to places where, during the war, bombs had been dropped but hadn't exploded. They had sunk deep into the ground, some in a river. We got wet and dirty, and it was dangerous work, but I took solace in the promise that I would soon be going home.

I looked forward to the day I could go home to Germany. We made so little money as POWs that I wondered how I would get a new start on life again. As I pondered, I came up with a plan to help me get on my feet once I arrived. Before my friend, Reinhardt, left for Germany, I made arrangement to send him parcels. He agreed to sell the contents. With the first money, he would send me German newspaper advertisements so I could look for a job. With future parcels, he would save the money for me when I arrived. The ads duly began to arrive.

I advertised for a job in West Germany, and after a time a dentist in Saarbrücken agreed to hire me when I was released. Things were looking up!

I missed my church family back in Lincoln. Since there was no Adventist church in Alford, sometimes on Sundays I went to the Methodist church. There, too, I made friends.

Occasionally, I took a bus back to Lincoln for the weekend. My friends still welcomed me and still gave me canned goods to send to my parents. One of those Sabbaths, a special weekend meeting for young people to be held in Nottingham was announced. There, I met a pastor who invited me home for dinner. Pastor Warland was full of life, loved to tell stories, and had an infectious chuckle. After dinner he asked if I would go with him to the sanatorium to visit his daughter, who had tuberculosis. She looked and spoke like her mother—dark hair, brown eyes, serious, and quiet.

But at dinner, there had been a younger daughter—Margaret. She had the blue eyes and ready laugh of her father. She showed no prejudice that I was German. Her sunny disposition attracted me—it seemed like everything I had not had for the last few years.

I got to know the family better on subsequent visits. Margaret and I obviously shared a mutual attraction. Communicating was a challenge, but with motions, slow speech, and a good helping of humor, we were getting to know each other. She seemed less mature than I in some ways. *That should be no surprise,* I reasoned. *I have experienced a lot.*

I spent a little money on bus trips to Nottingham but otherwise saved all the money I could. Besides continuing to send parcels to my parents, I used every cent I could to send goods to Reinhardt. The sales of the items I sent would add up to give me a good start when I arrived back in Germany. *Maybe I can marry before too many years—after all, I am twenty-seven.*

Here I was, dreaming again. It almost shocked me.

Finally, in the fall of 1948, I received a date for release. Immediately I wrote to the dentist to let him know when I could begin work. I busied myself making final arrangements. The dentist's reply came within weeks.

> I liked your resume and appreciate your responses. I am sure I would enjoy working with you. When I wrote you before, I fully intended to employ you. Unfortunately, money is so scarce that people come to the dentist only when they have pain. They don't come for crowns, bridges, or dentures. I barely do enough work to support my family. Until the economy picks up, I cannot hire another person.
>
> I am so sorry to have to give you this news.

My heart felt as though it had stopped in my chest. *Finally . . . after all these years . . . I am about to be free, and I have no place to go.*

No Place to Go
1948

So much for plans! What now?

I couldn't leave for Germany till I had work lined up. It was too late now to get work. I would no longer have a place to stay in England. Furthermore, POWs were not free just to stay if they happened to be so inclined. But there was one exception—to be hired for bomb disposal. Since I'd already worked on the crew and they seemed happy with my work, there was a chance.

I went after the papers and got the request in motion. But my application had a condition attached—I had to be allowed to take a month off early the following year to visit my parents.

Request granted. I signed a contract for one year, became a civilian, did bomb disposal under the military as before, and continued to live in a barracks. When the contract ended, it could be renewed for another year, or I would have to leave the country. I received minimum wage. First I had to save money to visit my parents and to get back.

I'd heard enough about different occupation zones in Germany to know it would be risky for me to enter the Russian Zone. Since I was born in Saxony and grew up in Silesia, they could easily keep me. To make application the legal way would take at least three months. It could take much longer. I could be denied or not be processed at all.

Returning prisoners from the Western Allies were suspect and had to go through a reeducation camp before they were released.

To be safe, I never wrote my parents that I would visit them. But I did tell them when I would visit an Aunt Olga in West Germany.

In February 1949, I took the train to the English coast and a ferry to Holland. The customs officer looked at my papers, which identified me as a POW, and made me stand aside. After everybody else had gone through, he allowed me to leave. Carrying my suitcase, I ran to catch the train, hopping on to the last coach as the train began to move. I was perspiring by then but glad to be on the train and not have to wait till the next one—the next day.

I stayed with Aunt Olga for two days. Since I planned to return to England, I couldn't afford to lose my papers. I left them with my aunt and boarded a train for Hof. Mutti had sent me the address of a church member in Hof.

I enjoyed watching the part of the German countryside that hadn't been bombed or burned. I was having a nice trip until we approached a major city and a soldier announced, "When the train stops, have your papers ready for inspection."

Papers? Inspection? I left my papers with Aunt Olga.

I swallowed hard. *What will I do?*

The soldier walked back to the next car. I hoped he hadn't noticed any change in my expression at the mention of papers.

What can I do? I wondered. I glanced around me.

Across the aisle was a young mother with whom I had spoken briefly. I leaned close to her. "Who checks tickets?" I asked, trying to sound casual. "And when?"

"A German ticket inspector with a couple of occupation soldiers checks while we are stopped at the station," she answered.

A plan started to form in my mind.

I leaned closer to her. "Madam," I said quietly, "I didn't know they checked papers here. I left mine with my aunt in Bremen. Would you tend my suitcase while we're at the station?"

Her brows creased. "Bu—" she started. She glanced around. *"Ja,"* she agreed.

I lifted my suitcase over to her, and she situated it behind her bag.

When the train stopped at the station, I hopped off the train and went to the toilet on the platform. I waited, listening. My heart pounded. I waited some more.

"Last call for Hof," a conductor finally called.

I waited a minute more. When I heard the train start to move, I ran out of the restroom and jumped onto the moving train.

The military police just stood there, watching.

In Hof, I looked up the family whose address Mutti had sent. The husband knew somebody who was a border guard and explained my situation. The guard had a question—"What can he give if we help him?" From England I had brought ladies' stockings, chocolate, and other valued items.

I followed the guard's instructions—"When it gets dark, he should walk toward the border. We will arrest him and take him by jeep to the border. Then we'll speak up for him that he's not involved in spying or smuggling but just wants to visit his parents after his release as a POW in England."

The night unfolded as scripted. At the border, two guards took me to a bunker with bunk beds with no mattresses. "Rest awhile," one said. "The best time to cross will be about two in the morning. We'll wake you." I knew people sometimes got shot as they tried crossing illegally. But my nerves were good and my conscience was clear. I stretched out on the board bunk and slept.

The guards woke me at two. "When you reach the forest, you'll come to a railroad line from which the rails have been taken," one of the guards said. "When you get there, you are on the other side."

"But don't take any train or bus when you come to the first towns," the other suggested. "They have people on the lookout for border crossers."

It was a cloudless night, the full moon glistening on half a foot of snow. With the snow in front of me, I'd be clearly visible. I stepped into the night. My heart pounded louder than my footfalls.

After about two hundred yards, I reached trees. My pulse eased a little.

Then, there was the railroad line with the rails missing!

Walking east, I came to a road, then to a village. It was about four in the morning, and people were already walking and a few bicycling to work. Between five and six, many were on their way.

I heaved a sigh of relief. I had slipped through the patrols that guarded the border and made it past the first villages. No one would stop me now from seeing my folks! I'd walked across Russia; I could walk all day and all night if I needed to. I felt like whistling, but it seemed the better part of wisdom to keep quiet.

Late in the afternoon I came to the sign that read, "Plauen." Since I'd never visited my folks in this city, I inquired for the street.

My heart raced again. My thoughts kept pace. *How will they really be? Sometimes in their letters I'm sure there was more between the lines. Are they as well as they say? Will I see Hannchen and Jo?*

Then I stood at their door. I rang the bell, and the door opened. There was Mutti. We fell into each other's arms. We could not speak. The moments . . . and more moments . . . overflowed with emotion. It wasn't so much the five years since we had seen each other but all that had happened.

As we relaxed, the words came in torrents.

After a while Mutti said, "Excuse me, please. I will be right back. I have to check the oven."

I watched her go. She seemed frail compared to what I remembered.

I heard an oven door clunk open. The fragrance of home baking reached me. I followed her into the kitchen.

"This morning," Mutti said, "I just knew you were coming today. I baked a *kuchen* to celebrate."

"It smells wonderful!" I said.

"And the table's set for you," she added, motioning toward the table. It was set for three.

Vater had gone to town. When he arrived home, the emotional greeting repeated itself.

We had so much catching up to do. Hannchen was teaching school in a nearby village. Jo taught in *gymnasium* in another town. Vater and Mutti and I each shared the tales of our own experiences. God had been so good to us! We *all* had survived the war.

Mutti's potato soup was thinner than I remembered. And the *kuchen* seemed different. After we ate, when I saw Mutti pull back the curtain over a cupboard, I suspected I knew why—she probably didn't have the usual ingredients. But she had put together what she could out of her near-bare cupboards.

What a celebration!

"Do be careful where you go and whom you talk to," Mutti pleaded the next morning as I was about to leave to walk around and see the circumstances of the city with my own eyes.

"*Ja,*" Vater added. "There's someone in every apartment block and every section of houses to watch and report what goes on."

Hannchen and Jo came over the weekend. They, too, were thin. There was so much more than what they could tell me in letters. The reeducation camp that Jo had to go through nearly starved him. He came out so sick that even a Russian doctor wrote him a release from working in the uranium mines where he had been assigned.

Hannchen and Mutti were so weak from starvation when they first heard from me that they could not sit up in bed. They started gaining strength when my parcels began to arrive.

A chill went down my spine.

"You are my Joseph," Mutti said, moisture glistening on her lower eyelid. "You went from home and you sent food back that saved our lives."

"It was our church members too," I said. "They brought me many of the things I sent."

"Do thank them!" Mutti urged. "Tell them we are much better because of their gifts!"

"I will!" I assured her.

I marveled—when it seemed through the months in an English POW camp that my life was accomplishing nothing, God had used me in ways I could not know. He had used the food my church friends and I had sent to save Mutti's and Hannchen's lives. Silently, I vowed to keep the parcels coming.

It didn't take many days to realize my appetite was a drain on my parents' allotment. Food was still scarce and rationed. Since I was there illegally, I couldn't apply for food stamps. Though they didn't talk about it, every day I sensed my parents' increasing concern for my safety.

After ten days I decided it was time to disappear again. When I told Mutti and Vater, they didn't discourage me from going.

"Be careful," Vater said. "You know there was a rumor that two men were shot the night you crossed on your way here."

Leaving wasn't easy during the war. It was no easier now.

We prayed together. I hugged and kissed them both.

"Do be careful," Mutti pleaded.

"I will," I assured her.

"We will be praying for you."

I left, midmorning, trying to look as though I was on an everyday errand. But I wondered, *Will I see them again?*

I hoped to cross at the same spot as before. I left the road and crossed the hills. About midnight I thought I was close to the border. Then I heard a voice. I barely had time to hide in a clump of bushes.

There came two guards with guns over their shoulders and an Alsatian dog on a leash. The dog looked my direction and barked. The guards stopped. They listened. They looked directly at the bushes that stood between us.

What Future?
1949

The guards looked and listened. The dog stood alert beside them, staring into the clump of bushes I lay in.

Nothing moved or made a sound.

They walked a few paces. Again, the dog barked toward me. The guards stopped and listened. The Alsatian looked my direction but did not pull on its leash.

All was silent till they moved on again. In a few feet, the dog looked my way again and barked. This was repeated several more times, until the guards came within twenty-five feet of me. I thought they could hear my heart beating. I hardly dared to breathe. They walked a few steps. The dog barked. When they stopped and listened, the dog stood silent too.

It seemed like an eternity before they moved on, but it was probably only twenty or thirty minutes. I waited till they were well past before I moved. Then I adjusted my course, moving away from them. Shortly, I noted the stars again and headed due west.

After walking for some distance, I came to a village I thought should be west of the border. To make sure, I went to a nearby farmhouse that still had light shining from the windows. "Hello," I called, "I need help." The lights turned off, and no one came to a window or door. A little farther on, another house still had a light on. The same thing happened.

I walked to the center of the village to the mayor's office. *Oh-oh*, I thought. The main words on the billboard were in Russian. Through the door I saw people carousing. The smell of cigarettes and liquor wafted to the street. I hurried on to the far end of the village and entered a small wood.

I had walked due west. Why was I not west of the border? Why hadn't I looked at a map again before I left?

A small branch snapped. I hid, listened, and watched.

Three people were moving through the trees. They came closer. I saw they were carrying rucksacks and bags in their hands. Apparently they had been in the west and returned loaded with food. When they were a few feet from me, I spoke.

They froze, dropping everything they carried.

"Don't be afraid," I said. "I want to go where you came from."

"Don't talk so loud!" one whispered. "This is a *very* dangerous corner."

They whispered directions to me.

I continued due west. When the morning began to dawn, I was in the west again.

As I walked, I thanked God for helping me hear danger in time, for the dog not pulling on its leash to lead the guards to my hiding spot, for my making it back to the west, and for my parents' prayers. Had I been depending on their prayers too much? Should I be talking to God more myself?

Aunt Olga, and my mother's friends who had helped me, praised the Lord for my safe return and wanted to hear all about my folks. We also looked at a map. It explained my midnight puzzle—the border made a pocket to the west, and I happened to walk into it.

After a couple of days' rest, I left to hunt up Reinhardt. I was eager to see how much money the food parcels I had sent him had brought. I was spending everything I had on this trip and needed that money.

I needed to get back on my feet when I got back to England, and I needed to send food to my family. They had little food when I left. It was critical that I mail a parcel right away and follow it with others very soon.

Reinhardt welcomed me to his home, but I sensed he was nervous. He introduced me to his wife, Inge, and their two children. Since he spoke some English, he had landed a job at an American base.

After we had visited a bit, I thanked him for sending the newspapers and broached the subject of the parcels I'd sent and the money he'd saved for me.

Sadness came over his face.

Out of the corner of my eye, I noticed that Inge's expression turned to ice.

"Georg," Reinhardt said, "I'm so sorry, but it's all gone." He swallowed as if to gain the composure to continue. "Sometimes we had no food when they came. I sold some things and tried to save the money, but it's gone. It's all gone."

I sat, stunned, for an instant.

Inge didn't give me time to gather my thoughts. "The nerve, for you to even ask for money!" she exploded. "We lived in Silesia. The whole area was given to Poland. We had to walk off—leave our business, leave our home, leave everything we couldn't carry in three suitcases. We lost everything. Sometimes we have no food to give our children. And you ask *us* for money?

"You are single," Inge ranted. "You don't understand how it is! You're by yourself. You can start over." Her eyes narrowed even more. "Besides," she sneered, "aren't you a Christian?" Inge looked me in the eye. When I didn't avert my gaze, she got up and left the room.

There wasn't much to say after that. I left. I had nothing to show for all the work, all the scrimping, all the times I had gone without something I really needed for the sake of my future. *What future?*

I had one more task to do before I left Germany—find out about my chances to immigrate to North or South America.

As I walked, I thought about the last few years. War began, we were told, to undo the injustice of the Treaty of Versailles after World War I. Instead of restoration and peace, it turned into more destruction—destruction worse than what followed the Treaty of Versailles.

Agreements had been made and agreements broken. Trust was slain in the war—trust between individuals, companies, and governments. Whole societies lay in rubble—their buildings, their relationships, their lives. All that was left now was survival, waiting, trying to hope. I wanted to turn my back on Europe.

The newspapers and the rumor mill were full of talk of the Morgenthau Plan—what I heard was that it called for Germany to become an agricultural country with few industries. Also, anyone who had lived under Hitler would not be allowed to immigrate to another country. Displaced people from other countries would be considered victims of Hitler and would be given first chance. Germans who had lived in territories given to Poland were also excluded from immigration. I was one of them.

Sometimes having money helped. I didn't. In most cases, also, the person wanting to immigrate had to have a relative or someone else in that country willing to sponsor them. I didn't.

"Don't even bother with trying to get into the United States," some had said. "Canada or South American countries are easier."

Though I feared to hope, I had to try.

Early the next morning I walked to the Canadian consulate in Bremen. Though I arrived an hour before they opened, hundreds of people were already waiting in line.

"How long have you been here?" I asked a man in front of me.

He looked at the rising sun. "Two hours, maybe," he replied. "Two hours . . . today."

"You've been here other days?"

"Ja," he replied. "Just three days, so far."

Men and women sat on the street or leaned against a building. Some tried to keep children in tow. Children cried.

The doors finally opened. The sea of bodies surged forward a few feet.

By midmorning we had progressed only a few feet more. I realized my getting to immigrate was hopeless.

I returned to England and the bomb disposal work. In some ways, we were a pitiful and homeless group left behind from various POW camps. Some had not only lost their homes and country but their whole families. The remaining Poles did not wish to return to a Communist Poland. Some of us chose not to go to the Russian Zone of Germany. Some married locals for convenience rather than love—so they would have some place to call home, and they could begin to rebuild their lives.

On my next visit to Nottingham, Margaret was interested in my trip to Germany. We talked some about our future.

Before I left, Pastor Warland called me aside. "Georg," he said, "I have a concern that Margaret should finish her education before making other serious plans for her future."

"Of course," I agreed. "I would want that also."

His eyes narrowed. His head turned slightly to the side. "But there are *years* ahead," he said. "She is only seventeen, you know."

My mouth dropped open. "Seventeen?" I questioned.

"Yes," her father assured me. "She is only seventeen."

Oh-h-h, my, I thought. *She was only sixteen when we met?* I could hardly believe it. *How did we miss talking about age?* I wondered. *I am eleven years older than she.*

Back at camp, I puzzled about what I should do about Margaret's and my age difference. I also looked for extra work to supplement my day job's minimum wage so I could continue to send parcels home and to start over saving, to get a start in whatever I might do with my life. I checked at the camp kitchen and started working at night or on my days off, washing pots and pans, peeling potatoes, or whatever else needed to be done. Eventually I learned enough broken English that I became a relief switchboard operator at the camp. Franz was one of the other operators. He had lost his wife in the war. Together, Franz and I took a three-month, one-evening-a-week class—English for Beginners. I was still pretty lost among true English speakers, but it made

the job of operator easier. With both jobs, it was easy to get someone to trade with me or work an extra shift if I'd been put on the schedule for Sabbath.

Since we were now considered civilians, Franz and I asked and got permission to live off the camp—we were tired of living with forty or fifty men in a bar-

Georg in England, no longer a POW, working as switchboard operator in a military camp

racks. A nearby farmer showed us a place over his house. It had a roof, a floor, and a ladder leading up to it. We placed our beds under the sloped roof. The center was high enough that we could stand up. The space had no electricity, heating, or toilet. One end had no wall. But it did have privacy! How we enjoyed that.

Then the bomb squad moved to Horsham. Again, there was no Adventist church. Sometimes I attended the Baptist church with Franz.

I still wondered what I should do about Margaret. Franz discouraged the friendship. "With eleven years difference," he said, "you will not have a fully satisfying relationship."

On one of my visits to Nottingham, Pastor Warland, concerned for me and my future, asked, "Georg, now that you are considered a civilian, have you ever thought of applying to Newbold College here in England?"

In the following days I pondered my future and prayed for God's guidance. He didn't bring any red flags to my mind. Every other avenue seemed to be closed to me. Was college God's answer?

I mailed an application. Pastor Warland wrote a letter of recommendation. I looked forward to the day I could bid bomb disposal goodbye and begin to rebuild my life.

But I would need money. Again, I looked for a second job. First I approached a dentist. He let me work evenings and any day I was available, even Sundays. He liked my work. Soon I did crowns, bridges, and other work with which his full-time technician was not familiar. At times he would call me in to see a patient he had in the chair and discuss with me the best way to solve a problem.

I bought a used bicycle to ride back and forth to work. Getting to and from work more quickly gave me more time *at* work. That meant more income. That translated into more savings for college. I appreciated the dentist. I appreciated the work and the income. But did I want to do this the rest of my life? What did I want to do?

The scholarship to dental school had gone up in flames with much of Germany. I wasn't interested in pastoring or teaching. What about being a missionary? Helping people in need sounded interesting to me. Giving the gospel, giving hope to people who had no other way of hearing it began to entice me.

Generally I worked for the dentist on Sundays. Occasionally I went to church with Franz, and then we went on some outing just to get away. One Sunday he arranged for us to go on a bus tour to an old residence of English kings. A group of girls from Switzerland were on the same tour, and one of them caught my eye. Her name was Helen. She had come to England to improve her English while being a nanny to the children of an army major. On the way home, the girls sang familiar songs in German that I hadn't heard since my youth. It was a wonderfully pleasant day of relaxing.

On some weekends I still traveled to Nottingham to see Margaret. As much as I enjoyed her company, I still questioned our age difference. And even if she'd been old enough so we could marry and I would be free to work as a dental technician, I wasn't sure that was really my calling in life. As I prayed about my future, being a missionary interested me more and more. Would I soon be able to go to college? The possibility thrilled me.

The college's response soon came: "There are many local and overseas students who need to work to pay their school fees. It is too soon after the war for us to be able to afford to take on the responsibility of a student who has no means of support."

I wandered outside and walked. Drizzle dampened my coat to match my spirits.

"God," I prayed, "is there ever going to be a door that opens for me?"

CHAPTER 30

Company
1950

The next time I went to visit Margaret, I took the letter from Newbold College and showed it to her father. After he read the letter, Pastor Warland didn't say a word—about it or anything else. He just sat there, head down. Several moments ticked by.

Finally he looked up. "Georg, if I were you, I would leave Europe."

"My thoughts exactly," I agreed. "But how?"

His eyes took on a thoughtful look. "Why don't you try going to Helderberg College, in South Africa?"

South Africa? That was a new thought to me. I had considered the United States and been discouraged. I would gladly go to Canada or Argentina. Actually, anyplace in North or South America. But South Africa?

Why not?

There were a few reasons why not: Germany didn't have a single consulate anywhere in the world. When would it be possible to get a passport and travel with it? And then, I would need a visa. And money to travel—that would take some doing.

"Well, God," I said the next morning, "here I am trying to play God again. Helderberg College seems desirable in some ways. But I surely don't see any way I could get there. Would You give me wisdom, please?"

Days went by—bomb disposal, dental technician work, passing Helen (the Swiss girl) from time to time as I rode back and forth to the dentist's office. I ignored her for six months. Even though I wasn't quite sure what to do about our age difference, Margaret was my girlfriend, and I loved her.

I continued to pray about Helderberg. One morning I told God, "I want to do whatever You have in mind for me. I've tried my own plans a number of times, and they don't work out so hot. But You know what is best for me. Unless You let me know something else, I will proceed on going to Helderberg College or to America. Whichever door opens first, I will consider to be Your leading."

One day a letter from Margaret's father arrived. He spoke of general news. Then he wrote: "Lately I have noticed Margaret getting chummy with a young man at church. I asked her, 'Do you think your friendship is fair to Georg?' She surprised me, snapping back, 'If I'm not allowed to date others, then I rather wish Georg would not come anymore.' "

Pastor Warland finished his letter by saying, "I remember, Georg, that you were engaged before, and it ended in great disappointment for you. I just wanted to warn you, so you might not experience the same disappointment again."

I sighed. I loved Margaret. But this letter seemed to confirm what I'd already been thinking.

There wasn't much going on in the small town of Horsham. Franz knew I wasn't interested in movie shows. Occasionally he came up with an idea of something to get me away from work, work, work. One Monday evening he convinced me to go to a local school for a program by the students.

The auditorium was almost full when we arrived. We found one row that had three empty seats. Franz sat at one end, and I sat next to him, beside the empty seat. Franz and I were talking when a sweet voice asked in German, "May I sit here?"

I turned to say *"Ja."*

Helen smiled and slipped into the seat.

I don't remember the play. But we whispered comments during the program and visited during breaks.

Before the applause at the end of the program had died down, Franz leaned toward me. "See you later," he said. He hopped up and was gone.

No problem. I walked Helen home. We weren't in any rush.

Later, Franz greeted me back at the barracks. "Have a good evening?"

"Yes."

Franz grinned. "Seeing her again?" he asked.

I smiled and nodded. "Wednesday evening."

His eyes twinkled . . . a little more than I expected.

My eyes narrowed. "Did you know Helen was going to be there tonight?"

His grin grew. "Ye-e-s."

I eyed him. "Was this a setup?"

"You've been avoiding her for so long," Franz said. "We just came up with a way to get the two of you together long enough to get acquainted."

"Can't say that I mind," I responded. There was a smile in my heart.

Now I really had a problem. I prayed. I walked and thought. I talked to Franz. I must break off my relationship with Margaret. I must let her know I would not be coming for Christmas. I wrote—as kindly and gently as I knew how.

I felt freer to enjoy Helen's company even more. I did, except for wondering about our religious differences.

Margaret shot a letter back as fast as mail traveled. "I love you," she wrote. "I cannot bear to think that I will not see you again. Please come for Christmas." She went on, expressing her love in ways I had longed to hear before.

I was beginning to really appreciate Helen's depth and maturity, but I also thought of my own earlier hurt and felt very sad for Margaret. *Did I make the best decision?* I wondered.

The first of December, I received a letter from Helderberg College. It ended, "If you can find your way to us in South Africa, we will accept you as a student."

The acceptance from Helderberg was like a shot in the arm. But . . . that little word *if* held major implications. How was I going to get there?

"God," I prayed, "I accept this as Your leading. But if this is Your plan, You're going to have to open some doors that are too big for me!"

I would need a passport and a visa. I would need money for those and for transportation to South Africa. My contract for work with the bomb disposal squadron would expire at the end of December. Renewal would obligate me for another year. If I didn't renew it and the visa took several months or was denied, I'd be in deep trouble.

"A step at a time," I seemed to hear God whisper.

Right then, the West German government was opening their first foreign consulate since the war, and it was in London. I applied for a passport just before Christmas. On Christmas Eve Helen and I attended a celebration at the new German consulate. My passport was one of the first few issued—number twenty-six. Now I could apply for a visa to South Africa.

With the bomb disposal contract, I requested a provision that I would be permitted to leave if I was granted a visa to go to South Africa. My request was granted.

Now I was even more motivated to work for the dentist as much as I could . . . but, also, to see Helen as much as I could.

She introduced me to her employer, and it was fine with both the mother and father if I visited Helen in their home, even when she was caring for the children. Their big house was like a villa in a park, with manicured lawns, shrubs, and trees. Sometimes we played with the children—Helen was good with them. They obviously respected and loved her. It was clear from their relationship with her that the kindness and love she showed me wasn't just superficial. It was truly her heart.

As we got better acquainted, questions came up from time to time. "No ham on your sandwich?"

"No thanks."

"You don't like ham?"

"I don't eat it because in the Bible pigs are listed among the animals God says aren't healthy for us to eat."

Helen's forehead furrowed. Her head tilted to the side as she turned toward me. "The Bible says it isn't healthy?"

"Right," I responded. "In Deuteronomy fourteen and Leviticus eleven, God told the people what meats would be OK to eat and what meats would be harmful."

"So, what is good and what isn't?" she asked.

I told her some of what the Bible texts said. She was amazed.

Another time, Helen asked, "So . . . why do you go to church on Saturday instead of Sunday?"

"The Ten Commandments talk about that," I said. "In Exodus twenty, one of the commandments is, 'Remember the sabbath day, to keep it holy. Six days shalt thou labour, and do all thy work: But the seventh day is the sabbath of the Lord thy God.' "

"But isn't Sunday the right day?" she asked.

"Not according to the Bible," I answered. "God always numbered the days of the week—first day, second day, third day, and so forth. Days weren't called other names until later. Pagan people worshiped many gods and named the days of the week after their gods. Sunday is the day set aside to worship the sun. But there was never sun worship for God's people. From the Garden of Eden, God was very specific about which day of the week was the day for special fellowship with

Him. Down through history that has always been the seventh day, the day we call Saturday."

The discussion was lopsided—though Helen was well read and was fully a part of most of our discussions, she had little knowledge of Scripture.

In February, an invitation to the South African consulate in London arrived. I needed to present myself for an interview.

The building was impressive, with its marble walls, high wooden doors, and high ceilings. A porter took me to a waiting room. For two hours I waited in its cold opulence by myself. The porter finally appeared again and motioned me to enter a door.

I stepped in. "Good afternoon, sir," I respectfully greeted the man behind the imposing desk.

The man behind the desk paged slowly through a folder. He did not speak. He did not look up. Eventually, still looking into the folder, he asked, "You want to go to South Africa to attend a Methodist college?"

"No, sir," I responded. "I want to attend a Seventh-day Adventist college."

He looked up at me. Raising his stern voice, he growled, "But you wrote you wanted to go to a Methodist college! How do you explain that?"

I knew good and well that I had not written Methodist. But what good would it do to argue? "I am sorry, sir," I replied. "I have no explanation for this. But I know I want to go to a Seventh-day Adventist college."

His eyes narrowed. "You can leave," he ordered.

Well, God, I prayed silently as I walked down marble steps, *obviously nothing's going to come of that. So . . . what's Your plan now?*

Chapter 31

Family?
1951

I didn't hear an answer about God's plan for me. I just went on working day and night—bomb disposal, dental projects, covering switchboard. Helen and I fit in a few wet, winter walks. We had several more religious discussions—for starters, the use of images in worship, praying to saints, and papal succession following Peter. Our religious differences bothered me, but every time we talked

Helen and Georg while dating in England

about it, Helen felt certain our love was enough to overcome whatever difficulty arose.

I kept talking to God about His plan for me; kept telling Him I was trusting Him to work out my future.

Two weeks went by. A thin envelope from the South African consulate arrived by post. *Don't need many pages to say "Request denied,"* I reasoned.

The enclosed letter included, "Your immigrant visa to South Africa has been granted. At your earliest convenience, please return to the consulate with your passport."

My head spun. *So, what happened? Had the consul just been testing me? How did God work this out?*

I didn't know *how* God worked it out. But it was very clear that now I had some planning and arranging to do.

"God," I said, "thank You for opening this door. I accept this as Your plan. Please keep leading me."

I went to tell Helen. She hugged me. "Georg, that's wonderful!" Then her eyes darkened. "It is . . ." she swallowed hard, ". . . but it isn't. South Africa is a long way off."

"But you can come too."

We started making plans.

I counted my savings and bought a ticket from Southampton, England. I wrote to Helderberg College telling them I would be visiting my family in East Germany and had booked passage to Cape Town, South Africa. I told them the date I'd arrive on the ship, *Sterling Castle.*

Helen resigned her job. We would visit my parents and hers, and then she would stay in Switzerland.

Watching the ads in the newspaper, I found two overseas trunks for sale and bought them for my voyage. I told my bosses that my visa had come, and I resigned from my various jobs. My coworkers started getting the news and congratulating me. More than once I heard, "Grellmann did it right. He worked and saved money. Now he can go overseas." I said Goodbye to the church friends who had welcomed an "enemy" into their hearts—they had given me hope when I had none and had been a part of saving my family's lives. What a sad, happy time. I packed a suitcase to take to Germany and Switzerland and packed the rest of my possessions in the two trunks and put them into storage.

Helen and I took the train to Brighton, a ferry overnight to Holland, then another train to Berlin.

My parents couldn't leave East Germany. If I went into East Germany, I probably couldn't leave. Berlin was the only possible place for me to see my family without fear of my being detained. At that point, Berlin was divided into sectors, but people could go back and forth within the city, knowing that whenever they entered or left the Russian sector, their papers could be checked.

As prearranged, Helen and I met my parents at rented rooms in West Berlin. It was a nerve-wracking delight. How good to see them again! But what would they think of Helen? How would they view our religious differences? I already had qualms about the difference, and they were sure to also. What would their attitude be?

Mutti and Vater were excited about my going to Helderberg College, thrilled about my decision to be a missionary. "But how can you pay for all this?" Vater asked.

"I have saved very carefully," I responded. "God has blessed."

"He worked all the time," Helen added. "At bomb disposal, as a dental technician, at switchboard. He works hard and is very careful to save. You must be very proud of him!"

"We are proud," Mutti agreed as she smiled up at me.

Later in the conversation, Vater looked at Mutti. "You are remembering you brought Georg something?"

"Oh, *ja, ja!*" Mutti exclaimed. She went to her suitcase then came back with a handful of papers and a small bag. First, she handed me the bag.

I opened it and looked in. I gasped. "How were you able to keep these?"

Vater smiled. "We wrapped them in plastic and buried them in the garden."

Helen was leaning, trying to see into the bag. I pulled out a small box and opened it. There were my bronze and silver medals. And my gold medal with the words *"Reichssieger 1939"*—National Winner 1939.

Memories flooded over me.

"We finally destroyed your certificate," Vater said. "If the new government officials had found that certificate with Hitler's signature, our whole family would have disappeared."

"I'm amazed you were able to keep these," I mused.

"We thought about giving them to you when you visited us in Saxony," Vater said. "But if you had been caught crossing the border and had your medals with the swastika with you, for sure you would have been considered a Nazi."

I raised my eyebrows. "That crossing was tense enough," I said. "Just thinking about it makes my heart pound. This was much safer!"

They had also brought my school records as I had requested.

Within a few hours, Mutti was trying to steer most every conversation onto religious themes. "Helen, why don't you study the Bible with Vater?" she urged. "I know he would be happy to study with you."

"Thank you," Helen tactfully responded. "We have too little time with you this visit."

We visited for a while, but before long, Mutti started talking about religion again . . . and again. Helen avoided the topic as much as possible. She conveniently needed to go to the toilet sometimes. Several times she tactfully declined. When she felt the pope or her church was being attacked, she defended them. That exasperated Mutti.

By the second night, after a short walk with Helen before she went to her room, Mutti expressed her frustration. "We are thrilled you want to be a missionary in Africa!" she started. "But here you come with a Roman Catholic girl. Do you remember the experiences we had in Upper Silesia? Do you remember the times Catholic boys jumped you? Do you know what we believe? How can you be a missionary if you marry someone who believes so differently from you?"

Mutti's questions were especially frustrating because I had thought the same thoughts a thousand times. And I didn't know the answers. I knew Helen was the kindest, most loving human being I had ever met. I knew she loved me more deeply than I had ever been loved. I knew I wanted to spend the rest of my life with her. But I also knew that, before we married, we had to figure out how we were going to handle spiritual issues.

Vater didn't say much about Helen's religious views.

Saying goodbye wasn't any easier than before. I was headed to Africa. To college, yes. But as far as I was concerned, I was going for life. This could well be the last time I would see my family.

I watched out the train window till I could no longer see the arms waving or the figures standing by the tracks.

I sat back in my seat and gave Helen's hand a squeeze. "Well, you survived meeting my family."

She grinned. An eyebrow rose. *"Ja."*

Helen's parents welcomed us to their home in a Swiss mountain village. The whole village was Roman Catholic except for the Protestant barber. Helen had already warned her family that I was Protestant.

The visit started out well. I felt accepted by Helen's parents. I got on well with her younger brother, who still lived at home, and her older sisters and their husbands, who lived nearby. I tried to make myself useful—I wasn't used to sitting around doing nothing. I noticed a truckload of firewood had been dumped in their yard. The second day of our visit, I stacked it in orderly piles in the shed. That evening Helen told me she had overheard her dad say to her mom, "This is the right man for Helen."

Encouraged, I approached her father the next day. "Herr Villiger, I haven't just come for a holiday. I am interested in your daughter."

He smiled. "I have already heard that you are Protestant," he said. "In matters of religion there are some differences. But between us as men, we can have some understanding. I can give you my approval as long as you agree to marry in the Catholic Church."

I knew there was more to it than that, but I wanted him to tell me. "The place of the wedding is probably not so important," I said. "Or does it have some significance?"

"Yes," he answered. "You must agree to have your children brought up in the Catholic faith."

I hoped we could discuss the subject in a gentlemanly way. I complimented him on the way he had brought up Helen. "But what if my parents expected from me what you are expecting from Helen?" I continued. "Shouldn't we have some say in it too?"

"I should have known!" he shouted. "Helen has always been a disobedient child. And now this!"

I hoped Helen couldn't hear his accusation, but considering his volume, it was likely she heard . . . loud and clear.

He went on and on, railing against his own daughter. When I thought he couldn't get louder, his bellow became a roar.

Eventually he wore down.

Helen's mother, youngest brother, and her sisters were embarrassed. All the women were crying. Even people in the street had heard the explosion. Helen had been listening outside the door and heard every defaming word.

"We must go," Helen insisted. We went up to our rooms, packed our suitcases, and left. Helen's older sister in Basel, who was also dating a Protestant, took us in. I went job hunting with Helen the next two days, and she accepted a job being in charge of the kitchen for a Jewish family.

I found the address for the Seventh-day Adventist church in Basel and invited Helen to visit with me on Sabbath. She went willingly and participated reverently through the service.

"It didn't seem like church," she said on the way home. "It seemed very strange."

"I'm not surprised," I said. "I'm sure if I went to the Catholic Church it would seem strange to me too."

She asked a few questions. I answered them with Scripture. I didn't push her, but I did suggest she read the Bible and study some Bible lessons.

The few days in Basel raced by too quickly. Leaving Helen behind tore my heart apart. She had promised to marry me; yet, questions nagged at me.

Within two days, I was back in England. I picked up my trunks, headed to Southampton, and embarked on my journey to South Africa. I settled myself in a shared cabin on the lowest deck with no porthole—that was the least expensive way.

At night I would go up on deck and look at the stars. The twelve-day voyage gave me time for almost more reflection than I could handle. *I hurt Margaret—that bridge is burned. I love Helen. But what will we do about the spiritual differences? Our parents are all concerned. Her father condemned our relationship.*

I'm going alone into a culture I don't understand. With limited funds.

I have an eighth-grade education. I haven't studied in school for fifteen years. I don't speak English well, and I don't read it at all. And I am enrolling in college?

Chapter 32

The Depths
1951

Alone on the ship's deck with only dreams to hold me, the impossibilities I faced taunted me. For some time, I looked up at the stars and thought about God keeping the universe.

"God," I finally whispered, "my little part of the universe may be pretty small to You. But it is looking very large to me. I need You to help me trust that You can handle it."

Memories of the war years rolled through my mind like a movie.

God hasn't forgotten me, I remembered. *It isn't just happenstance that I am alive when millions died. For some reason, He protected me over and over again.*

I sighed deeply. "God, the war took ten years of my life. I wore its uniform. I obeyed its orders. The rest of my life is for You!"

In the daytime I also spent a lot of time on deck. I visited with various people. One personable young couple from Rhodesia (now Zimbabwe) had just married in England and were on their way home. The acquaintance was warm until the husband got curious about my accent. "Where are you from?" he asked.

"Germany," I answered.

"I certainly hope that not many Germans come to Rhodesia," the wife retorted.

My heart fell. *Will every German be identified with war and the holocaust for the rest of his life?* I wondered. *How will I be accepted in South Africa?*

Shortly, the conversation ended, and I walked to the back of the deck. Alone, I watched the wake.

For some time now, I had understood what Hitler did to the Jews—the holocaust. I hated it as much as anyone. Maybe more than most, since I had fought in the German army. Was I somehow responsible in a minor way for Hitler's aggression?

I cried out to God again. "Forgive me, God. For every bullet I shot. For the injury to every person I hurt. For the pain I caused to families of the fallen."

Water churned in the ship's wake. The storm in my soul was deeper, wider, and stronger.

"Forgive me for not understanding why I fought. For condemning the Jehovah's Witness man who loved peace enough to lay down his life rather than fight. He was no coward.

"Forgive me for not valuing Your holy day enough to stand up for it. For drinking that one night. For stealing the chicken. For hurting Margaret."

I grasped the rail. My mind went back, back. I cried out for forgiveness for stealing the coin from Grandfather, for pranks. I confessed every sin I could think of. I finished, "Forgive me . . . for . . . for not knowing You!"

"I have," God seemed to say. *"I have thrown all your sins into the depths of the sea."*

The depths of the sea? I thought. I looked out over the ocean—left, right, ahead, behind. As far as I could see in any direction, there was nothing but sea. I looked down. I couldn't see into the water—I could only imagine its depth. In my mind, I could almost see God's big right hand holding all the evil I had ever done. I could see Him close His fist around my shame, lift His arm up and back, and heave my guilt into the water. In my mind, I heard the bundle splash and visualized it sinking . . . sinking . . . sinking.

Peace washed over me. I noticed a patch of blue sky in a break in the clouds.

Grace, I thought. *This is what grace is! And God gives it freely!*

"I want to know You better!" I said. "I'll take every theology class I can. I want to know You as *my* God, not just my parents' God. And I want to be totally open to Your plan for me."

I left the stern at peace. Would there be rough times ahead? Most likely. But the Savior who stilled the sea when He walked the earth could still my soul if I let Him.

We arrived in Cape Town at night. The ship went into dock. With sunrise, Table Mountain's green slopes rose above the city. I went through immigration and customs then stood there alone, looking around for someone from Helderberg College who had come to get me. No one showed up.

Finally, I inquired how to get to Helderberg College. The town closest to the college was Somerset West, about forty miles from Cape Town. I took the train and arrived early that afternoon.

Very few people got off the train at the small town. Soon the station was deserted. To save my pennies, I left my trunks at the station and walked two hours up the hill toward the college. It seemed all bridges behind me had been demolished. This was definitely more uncertainty than adventure. Quietly, I kept praying—for assurance, for strength, for faith.

When I arrived at the college administration building, a receptionist showed me to the president's office. "Georg Grellmann is here to see you," she announced.

Shock filled his eyes. He stood and reached out his hand. "Georg Grellmann," he finally said. "I am happy you have made it here."

"Thank you," I responded.

"I am amazed you are here," he said. "We knew from your correspondence that your parents live in East Germany. When you said you would visit them before you came, I fully expected you would be detained and not allowed to leave."

We discussed my situation. Most college freshman straight out of high school were required to work ten hours a week. With the language challenge, for me schoolwork would consume considerable time. And, certainly, I was acquainted with work. The college waived the work requirement, and I deposited my savings with the school to be withdrawn or cover schooling expense as needed.

Shortly, I visited with the registrar. I gave him my school reports and certificates. After paperwork and more discussion, he said, "Since you want to be a missionary, you'll need to take the four-year normal course."

I didn't really want to take teacher's training. I wanted to take theology, but I didn't want to be a pastor. I wanted to be a missionary. I followed his direction and signed up to take teacher training.

"We are just beginning second quarter," he said as we finished the enrollment process. "You may have some difficulty since you missed first quarter. Semester examinations will test on what was covered in both first and second quarters."

As if I don't already have enough to worry about! I thought. I chose not to stay with that line of thinking. *God,* I prayed silently, *this is too big for me. I am counting on You.*

A messenger took me to the train station to get my trunks, and later the boy's dean showed me to a room.

Life became regimented again—wake-up bell, worship bell, breakfast bell, class bell . . .

I was an odd duck around campus—at least ten years older than most students. I had picked up enough conversational English that I could follow most of what was said in class, but reading and writing was another story. Since English isn't a phonetic language, I had a hard time spelling words and looking up their meaning in a dictionary. While other students wrote page after page, I wrote a few sentences. Objective tests were much easier for me than essay questions!

Passing a spelling test and the first year College English class were required to be able to continue in school. The teacher was strict and demanding. I worked hard and prayed hard. I passed . . . with the lowest grade I had ever earned in any class. I was just thankful to be through with it!

I passed all my first semester exams, but it must have been by grace alone.

I prayed that God would help me make it through the assignments of the day, that He would help me learn, help me make passing grades, help me be able to cover my costs. There was a reason for my being at Helderberg College. I wanted to be a missionary, to introduce people to the good God I was getting to know better. I prayed often that God would prepare me to be the most effective missionary for Him that I could be.

One morning God spoke strongly to me through Isaiah 57:15: "For thus saith the high and lofty One that inhabiteth eternity, whose name is Holy; I dwell in the high and holy place, with him also that is of a contrite and humble spirit, to revive the spirit of the humble, and to revive the heart of the contrite ones."

The God who is holy, who fills heaven and eternity, I thought, *wants to fill me. He wants to revive me. When I am so tired that it seems I cannot go on, when I am so confused by English words and phrases it seems I will never understand, when I am so lonely for my loved ones that my heart is breaking, He wants to fill me with new life, new vigor, new strength, new courage, new hope.*

"But do I have Your humble spirit?" I asked. "And . . . is there anything more I need to repent of?"

A sense of needing to make everything right came over me. "God," I prayed, "I want to be right with You in *every* thing. I don't know of any sins I haven't confessed. Is there something else?"

In the silence, I knew there was more I needed to do—I needed to be right, not just in the eyes of God, but also in the eyes of those I had wronged. Over the next few weeks I wrote a variety of apologies. Some I didn't hear back from, some I did. Margaret forgave me. So did Pastor and Frau Schaller. The police in Lincoln regretted that from my description they couldn't identify the farm from which I had stolen the chicken, and therefore they were returning my payment to me.

Another thing nagged at me—while in England, I had not returned tithe on the wages I received. *If I don't take out tithe,* I had reasoned, *I can send more food to my family.* So I had purchased items to send and asked Mutti to tithe for me on the things I sent to them.

Mutti had done so. But I knew there was more. I figured my wages for the three years in England and then the amount of tithe I had not given. I sighed. *If I pay that now, it will run my savings dangerously low,* I thought. *Maybe I should wait until I am out of school and making a living wage.*

"No!" I answered out loud. "It is right! And I will do it now!"

Yes, money was tight. I struggled. But I was doing right . . . and a clear conscience is a wonderfully pleasant companion.

I prayed often for God to live in me, to revive me. I felt Him doing so. His friendship was precious. But even when He walked and talked with Adam in the Garden of Eden, He said it wasn't good for man to be alone, and I agreed with Him. I missed Helen terribly and set out to find out what it would take for her to be able to join me.

Because we were planning to marry, Helen could get a six-month visa. The government of South Africa would require a deposit in the amount of her return fare in case we didn't marry in that time. At the college, I asked about work. Yes, the college would hire Helen. They also had several small houses for married students, and we could live in one when we married.

But worries needled me. *Should I ask her to come? Even if I could figure out a way to earn the money, what about our spiritual differences?*

Sabbath afternoons were the only time I had to write letters. I wrote to Helen most weeks and sometimes to my family. Receiving replies were the highlight of my life . . . usually. In one letter from Helen, she said a pastor from the Seventh-day Adventist church had come to visit her and tried to get her to study the Bible with him. "I just didn't feel at ease with him," she wrote, "so I didn't invite him back." My heart sank.

Helen wrote of her work. She seemed to be getting on well with the Dryfuss family. I couldn't help wondering what she thought of their use of "clean" meats and of their day of worship.

A couple of weeks later my mother wrote that she had written the pastor in Basel and asked him to have Bible studies with Helen if possible. He wrote back after some time saying he had failed to arrange any studies because he couldn't detect any interest. "Georg," Mutti wrote, "if you are going to be a missionary, you must be married to someone who will support you in that."

Mutti had been so obnoxious in trying to get Helen to study the Bible that I could understand why Helen objected. I knew Mutti was right about the importance of husband and wife sharing the same spiritual values and vision. *But,* I questioned, *how can I tell Helen I can only love and marry her if . . .* My pulse pounded in my temples. *Impossible!*

My heart felt as though a spade had been dragged through it—ripping, tearing, shredding.

God, what must I do?

I heard no answer. I kept studying. School was getting easier—though I still had to work long hours to understand and to complete my assignments. I loved learning. One of my teachers invited me to join a group of young men who preached in nearby churches on Sabbath afternoons. I enjoyed participating and looked forward to the day when I would graduate from college and become a full-time missionary. Except that when I thought about that, disturbing thoughts left me feeling unsettled. *What will I do?* I wondered. *Will Helen ever show interest in the things I believe?*

And, just in case I didn't have enough to think about, the business manager gave me more. "Brother Grellmann," he said, "you are running out of funds. Unless you figure out a way to get more, you will need to drop out of school."

Quit?
1951

No! my thoughts screamed. *I can't quit now!*

"So, God, what do You have in mind?"

Student wages were even lower than minimum wage. If I tried to work at the school, I could never pay for tuition, meals, and living in the dormitory—let alone have time to go to class or study. Why not look again for work as a dental technician?

A dentist in Somerset West agreed to let me work evenings. He was an immigrant from Northern Ireland, and I got the sense he was glad to help another immigrant get a new start in life. I purchased a second-hand bicycle and proceeded into the quarter at school. Each weekday, after classes, I hopped on my bike and flew down the hill to town. I worked till 10:00 p.m.—or later, if there was some pressing need. On the night commute, I pushed the bike nearly all the way back up to the college. I generally arrived a little before midnight. At that point, I hadn't touched my homework. The days were hectic, but I managed to keep up with both schoolwork and bills.

On one midnight trip up the mountain when I was especially tired, I thought about family—my immediate family, the aunts, uncles, and cousins I had visited on my teen bicycle trip, and Grandfather. Suddenly, I felt again the knot in my stomach, as when I had pocketed his coin. Guilt filled me. Visions of other misdeeds paraded through my mind. *What makes me think I could ever be a missionary?* I questioned. *I have been part of . . .*

I stopped my bicycle and stood up straight. Looking into the black sky, I asked, "God, that's all been forgiven, hasn't it?"

A still, small voice whispered, *"Yes."*

I thought about the night on stern of the *Sterling Castle*. *"Thrown into the depths of the sea."*

"Yes."

"I praise You for Your forgiveness, God!" I said. Peace returned. I pushed the bicycle with renewed energy as I hummed a tune I'd learned in England. I thought about the words:

Georg shortly after arriving in South Africa

> Amazing grace! How sweet the sound,
> That saved a wretch like me!
> I once was lost, but now am found,
> Was blind, but now I see.

When I reached the dormitory, I had the energy and the peace to focus on studying.

The problem with Helen was not as easily solved. I prayed all the time that Helen would want to study the Bible, that she would see the beauty of friendship with the God I was getting to know. But as far as I could tell, nothing was happening.

Finally I could stand the pressure no longer. Sabbath morning I got up early. I walked up the mountain above the college, kneeled by a log, and prayed, "God, I have to know what to do about Helen."

As the sun rose, a jumble of thoughts fought for supremacy—the religious discussions Helen and I had had, Mutti's insistence that Helen study the Bible, Helen's resistance to Mutti, her defensiveness when she felt her church was being attacked, Mutti's pressing me to forget Helen, my love for her, and her deep love for me.

"No, God," I said. "I did not come up here to rehash what Mutti or Helen wants. Not even what I want." I swallowed hard, trying to hold back tears. "God, I want to know what *You* want!"

Golden light began to reach into the valley as I waited for God to speak. Finally, I sensed Him asking, *"Are you just asking for information? If you know, what will you do?"*

My heart felt as though it was being stretched . . . like a taut balloon that might explode any instant. I couldn't bear to lose Helen. Her love meant everything to me. All my dreams included her, and hers included me. How could I break her heart? How could I live without her?

Sometimes my thoughts raced by in bunches. Sometimes they seemed to plod, a word or a phrase at a time.

The silence wore long. Finally, it was as if I heard God ask again, *"Are you just asking for information? If you know, what will you do?"*

I clung to the log. "God, I-I-I . . . No, God. I cannot let her go."

All was still for a long time. I thought about how precious God was becoming to me. About how He wanted only what was for our best—everybody's—Helen's and mine. About how He could see from before the beginning of time until after its end. I saw Him sending angels to surround me on the Russian battlefields. I sensed again the forgiveness when He hurled all my sins into the ocean— His peace, His love, His joy. "No, God," I cried. "I cannot let *You* go."

I wiped the sweat off my forehead with my shirt sleeve.

"God," I offered, "I want Your will . . . no matter what it costs."

I sat back and leaned, exhausted, against a boulder behind me.

"I am not just asking for information, God," I said after several minutes. "Whatever Your plan is . . . if You will let me know what it is . . . in Your strength . . . I will do it."

In the stillness of that Sabbath morning a plan developed—"I commit to follow God. I will be a missionary. I will honor God before Helen. I will invite her to come to South Africa on a six-month visa. I will marry her only if she comes to love God and Bible truth, only if we share a commitment to God first. I will pray, pray, pray that she will study the Bible, but I will not push her to accept what I believe."

That afternoon I wrote to Helen. I explained about the visa, suggested she start on the paperwork, and told her that, with my dental technician job, I would be able to save and pay the deposit the government required to cover costs of her return.

Things were looking up. My heart was at peace with God, and I was committed to His plan for my life. I'd made a decision about Helen. The dentist seemed happy with my work, often staying after his workday to visit with me as I worked.

Then one evening, after about two months, he came into the lab after his appointments. "Georg, I got bad news today."

I couldn't imagine what bad news he would have gotten that he wanted to share with me.

"I talked to a labor union official today," he said.

"Yes?"

"He said you have an immigrant visa. Right?"

"Yes."

"He said that you can be either a full-time student or a full-time worker, but you cannot do both. You can work for me, all right, but then you cannot go to school. He said you would have to pick one or the other. You cannot do both."

"Choose?" I asked. I scratched my head. "If I don't work, I can't afford to go to school."

"I understand," he said. "But I'm kind of between a rock and a hard place. If I don't abide by their rules, we will both be packing."

So, with one labor union official's words, I was back to wondering how God was going to keep me in school.

I heard that some students would sell books during the summer vacation—November to February. Before the school year ended, the publishing secretary of the union came to conduct a workshop for student canvassers. I put my name in and attended. The leaders assigned me to an area that included two small villages in the Eastern Cape—Cathcart and Stutterheim.

Just before the school year ended, at the end of September, Alfred and Ruth Matter came to look me up. They were on a coastal furlough from Central Africa and had heard about a German student who attended college at Helderberg. Alfred was Swiss and Ruth from Germany. They had become engaged just before the war started. With the war and destruction, it seemed that they might never get together again. Others encouraged them to forget each other and get on with their lives. But for six long years, with no mail service between them, they had waited for each other. Now they served in Africa together and were glad to meet a German and speak their native tongue.

I enjoyed a number of hours with Alfred and Ruth while I was trying to firm up summer plans. To earn enough for a scholarship, I would need to put in many hours. Helen's ship was due to arrive the day before Christmas. My territory was eight hundred miles to the east, and the mode of transportation I could afford was hitchhiking. I needed to get to my area as soon as possible. One day I asked Alfred and Ruth, "Would you be willing to meet Helen when she arrives in Cape Town?"

"Of course we will," they agreed. "And she can stay with us until you get back and can make other arrangements."

I wrote Helen with the plan. I wanted desperately to meet her when she arrived, but I had no one to sponsor me. My parents were behind the Iron Curtain and, even if they had some money left, their currency couldn't be used in the West and had only one-seventh to one-fifth the value of the West German mark. My future depended on a scholarship.

I started hitchhiking as soon as I could get away from school in November. Summer was just beginning. Besides the samples of books I would sell, I carried one extra white nylon shirt, a set of underwear, toothbrush, soap, and a towel. At night, unless a family invited me to stay in their home, I slept under the sky.

When I reached my assigned area, the publishing secretary who was to meet and train me had not yet arrived. I walked around the village to look at the situation. I noticed five small red brick railroad houses. They seemed to be in the poorest section of the village. Going to a tree for shade, I prayed for courage and success. Then I went to the first house and received a book order. I came out of the third house with another order. The ice seemed to be broken. From then on I went to every house without much hesitation. On the third day the publishing secretary arrived. From one house to the next, we took turns giving the canvass. That evening he said, "You are doing fine. I am going to go on to my next appointment in the morning."

My case of books got heavier as the sun got hotter. I talked with many interesting people—pastors and paupers, native South Africans and German settlers, laborers and politicians. One woman's eyes narrowed when she recognized my German accent. "Because of you Germans," she spewed, "the world is still upside down."

Das Vorurteil, I thought. In an instant two situations flashed through my mind. First, the Rhodesian woman on the *Sterling Castle* who hoped not many Germans would come to her country—she had judged a whole group without knowing us as individuals. Second, a comment Helen had made in a recent letter. She wrote that she was getting on well with the Dryfuss family and then added, "Frau Dryfuss told me the other day that when she heard your high German, she almost didn't hire me because you were obviously from Germany." Helen went on to add, "Over the years, prejudice has caused so much hurt." *Prejudice lurks in many places,* I thought. *I will not let this woman's prejudice affect my attitude.*

But, sour as this woman sounded, before she could close the door on me, a voice from inside said, "Who is it? Let him in. I want to see him."

The woman ushered me in to visit with a man in a wheelchair. He was a retired school principal. We started a conversation, and the subject of war came up. "I shot German soldiers during World War I," he said. "We are *all* wrong!"

I agreed.

Tears came to the man's eyes. "As a German, would you forgive me for what I did to your people?"

"I forgive you," I said. "But, more importantly, God will forgive you!"

I received many orders as I went door to door. God was working. But as Christmas approached, I wished He would work faster—I still had a long way to go to earn a scholarship. And I had knocked on every door in the two small towns in my territory. I wrote to the Cape Conference requesting new territory. Church members invited me to go to the coast with them over Christmas to cool down and enjoy the ocean. I knew, with Helen arriving in Cape Town, I could not enjoy a vacation on the east coast. I decided to keep working so I could earn my scholarship as quickly as possible and get back to Helderberg to see Helen.

With my town territory covered, the only thing left to do was go into the country. In the summer's worst heat I rode a borrowed bicycle to the farms around the area. They were many miles apart. At farm after farm, no one was home. Late afternoon of the second blistering-hot day, I came to a farm where the owners had not yet left for the Christmas holiday. They didn't buy books, but they invited me to spend the night in their home. "I wish you a merry Christmas," the farmer said the next morning as he waved goodbye. Then, with a smile, he added, "With a nice girl."

That was enough for me. Helen would arrive in Cape Town that day. *What good am I doing here?* I reasoned. I returned the bicycle and hitched a ride west, arriving back at Helderberg College on Christmas Day, one day late to meet Helen at the pier. When I showed up at the Matters' door, Helen and I fell into each other's arms.

Christmas was wonderful, just being together. There was so much to catch up on. We both avoided religious topics. To not know how God was going to lead was difficult. I wanted to just say, "Let's get married." But I knew we did not yet share a commitment that would give us the foundation for true oneness. We were not yet ready to be effective and trustworthy servants of God.

Since I didn't yet know where I would be selling books, Helen didn't have work or a place to stay, and Alfred and Ruth were leaving to teach a class at a youth congress over the Christmas holiday at Hartenbos Camp near East London. They suggested we go along.

The trip with Helen and Alfred and Ruth was much more pleasant than hitchhiking many of the same roads. Whether we were driving, eating, or fueling up the car, much of the time when I was not specifically involved in a conversation, I prayed for Helen. *Will I have to send her back?* I sometimes wondered. Just the thought tied my stomach in knots. *Could I send her back?* I questioned. *Is there any way to compromise?*

The instant compromise entered my mind, I knew it could not be.

I prayed constantly that God would reach Helen's heart. Late one night I spent another painful session with God. In the end I vowed, "God, I give up my own plans for Yours. I will not marry Helen unless she comes to love You and Bible truth. I will not push her to accept what I believe. But I ask You to *plee-ease* help her see Your beauty. I trust Helen to You. But, no matter what it costs, I recommit to follow You."

Committed
1951

Many activities were available at the Youth Congress. Helen jumped right in and participated in the activities—she earned two Pathfinder honors, regularly attended events, and sang along as she learned the songs. She seemed to enjoy the meetings and even made some comments about God that surprised me. We enjoyed much of our time together, but we also attended some classes and activities separately. At night she went to a section of tents reserved for girls, and I went to the boys' section. As had become my habit, I prayed for Helen almost constantly.

The last Sabbath of the Congress, a baptism was scheduled. I had wished Helen would at least ask some questions about baptism. She had asked me none.

When time for the baptismal service came, we walked to the beach together. Hand in hand, we joined our voices in the singing.

After a few gospel songs, a pastor made his way to water's edge. "Will those who have prepared for baptism, please join me now."

I noticed several young men and women start toward the front. Helen gently pulled her hand out of mine. Without looking back, she walked to the water's edge.

I couldn't believe what I was seeing. Tears streamed down my cheeks. My heart wanted to sing. As the pastor read the baptismal vows, I thought I heard Helen's voice say a hearty "I do," agreeing with each tenet of faith.

Joy filled Helen's face when she came up out of the water. When she joined me again, her smile was as big as I had ever seen it.

Later that afternoon, Helen and I walked down to the beach, sat on a log and talked. "Why the decision to be baptized all of a sudden?" I asked her.

She smiled. "It wasn't as sudden as it seemed. I've been asking Ruth a lot of questions."

"Really?"

"Yes." Helen sighed. "From the very first," she said, "it always bothered me that when we got into a discussion about religion, you had answers from the Bible, and I didn't. When your mother started pushing, I resisted. But when my dad had no answers for you, and only anger, it really made me wonder. I wanted answers. As I talked with Ruth, I sensed she had answers too. So I started asking questions. Her answers made a lot of sense—just like yours did. Sometimes she showed me things in her Bible. Then, for the last couple of weeks here, I studied in the baptismal class."

"Why didn't you tell me you were going to the baptismal class?" I asked.

Helen looked into my eyes. "I didn't want to raise false hope," she said.

Tears welled up in my eyes. She reached over and squeezed my hand.

"Spending time with Alfred and Ruth," she continued, "I saw what went on in their home. I saw the oneness in spiritual things. I want that." Helen swallowed hard. "And I knew we could not have that unless we both were totally committed to the same thing."

I reached over and wiped a lone tear off her cheek.

"I didn't tell you I was studying because . . ." Her voice trailed off as she looked for words. "Because . . . I knew that if I studied the Bible and still did not believe as you, I would have to go back to Switzerland. You want to serve God, to be a missionary. If I couldn't throw my support behind you one hundred percent, it wouldn't be fair to you for me to stay. I figured that if I told you I was studying in the baptismal class and, in the end, I decided I was against what you believed, it would only be harder—harder for me to be honest with myself, harder for both of us to let each other go."

Tears streamed down our faces.

"At first it was a struggle to know if I was being honest with myself. But as I saw God in you, in Ruth, and in the people here, He became beautiful to me." Helen's eyes glowed behind the dampness. "I was always kind of frightened of God before. Now that I know Him better, I *want* to serve Him!"

I squeezed Helen's hand. We sat in silence for some time. Finally, I broke the spell. "The angels are singing," I said.

Helen with Pastor D. M. Baird, the pastor who baptized her

She smiled up at me. *"Ja,"* she said. "Rejoicing . . . over a lost daughter come home."

The song in my heart raised its pitch a note higher. It sounded vaguely familiar. Like the "Hallelujah" chorus?

Helen and I enjoyed our new commonality. It thrilled me to talk about spiritual things with her, to pray with her.

While at Youth Congress, I also received my new assignment for selling books—Queenstown. It was a good thing I had brought my case along, as it was only about a hundred miles from Camp Hartenbos. My heart ached when Alfred and Ruth drove off with Helen as their passenger.

I had all the more reason to work hard now—the sooner I earned my scholarship, the sooner I could go back to Helderberg and Helen. I started as early in the morning as seemed prudent and worked till as late as lights in the houses invited me to knock on their doors.

I continued to pray for Helen's spiritual growth. And, yes, I dreamed.

As soon as I was positive I had sold enough books to qualify for a scholarship, I stood on the side of the road with my thumb out again.

The reunion was wonderful. What a delight to pray with Helen and talk heart to heart about the most important things to us, to see her enthusiastically taking part in Sabbath School and mission opportunities. Helen spoke up for her understanding of the Bible in various situations, including some where her ideas would not be popular. But she spoke with such joy and peace that her words were generally well accepted. I was amazed at the depth of some of her answers. Others, also, saw her dedication.

Wedding day—Helen and Georg

Our love grew deeper, our fellowship sweeter. It became clear that Helen loved God with all her heart and was committed to serving Him with her whole life . . . no matter what it cost.

We had a small wedding. Alfred Matter stood up with me, and Ruth with Helen. The one sadness was that not one member of either of our families could be there.

After the simple ceremony, my history teacher helped us load a mattress on top of his small Austin car. We loaded the vehicle with food for a week and with bedding, and then he drove us to a state park in the Ceres Mountains. Five cabins overlooked a crystal clear river. We chose one and were alone. We didn't see another person all week.

Daytime, we enjoyed the scenery, the trees, and the birds. At night we listened to the orchestra of insects. Our souls and minds drank deep from each other. The moon enjoyed its many reflections in the water, inviting us to join them. We swam anytime we wished—summer had warmed the water till the temperature felt just right.

Wedding day—Alfred and Ruth Matter, Henry Smuts, Helen, Georg, Elder Thomas, who married them, and another Helderberg teacher

We felt as our first parents could have felt in their garden paradise—no guilt, no shame, just the beauty of deep love shared exclusively. Life felt like poetry. We felt close to God, to each other, and with the nature surrounding us.

Much too soon, the little Austin showed up again to take us back to the hard realities of life. For starters, the last married student house, which we had understood we could move into, had been given to a South African couple. Helen and I had each other, but we had no roof to cover our heads.

CHAPTER 35

Home
1952

Homeless. Together Helen and I told God the situation and asked for His leading. What a joy to face the challenge as a united trio—God, Helen, and me.

Through an ad in a Cape Town newspaper, we found a fourteen-foot camper for sale—the price was right because its roof and floor were rotted out. Alfred and Ruth came to our rescue again. Having just purchased a new pick-up, they pulled the trailer to my history teacher's backyard. We parked it under a fir tree, next to a small concrete building originally intended for a servant. Since the little building had a faucet and a room big enough for a table, we used it as a kitchen.

Georg and Helen's first home, with Helen in front. Their first child is in the carriage. Helderberg Mountain is in the background. Helderberg College is part way up the mountain, behind the large pine tree on the left.

Helen worked full time in the college kitchen, then the laundry. Though she wasn't a student, she was paid student wages. She came home with barely enough money to cover our food, week to week. Through my first quarter, I worked at repairing the trailer. By the time the first rain came, we were secure.

Next to the concrete building was room enough for a small garden. I dug out the grass, and the garden produced vegetables abundantly. That freed up a little money for other necessities. Every kettle, plate, or towel we bought was an accomplishment for which we were grateful. Supplies were meager; our love and happiness abounded.

The months slipped by. Helen worked, and I studied. Making friends came naturally to Helen, and she loved to entertain. On many Sabbaths we shared our simple dinner with guests.

The next summer I went canvassing again, leaving my pregnant wife at home. When I got a telegram that she had been taken to the hospital, I headed home immediately. When I walked into her room, baby Heinz was already in her arms. My eyes filled with tears as I looked back and forth between the two dearest ones in the world to me.

Every summer I canvassed. With the Lord's blessing, every summer I received a scholarship. The summer before my senior year another telegram alerted me that Helen was headed for the hospital. Again, I hitchhiked back there as quickly as possible. Again I was late. But I was no less thrilled with baby David.

After graduation, the four of us traveled back to Europe. I had gone to Africa by myself thinking I might never see my family again. I had tried God's promises. I had received His grace. I had been blessed with life and love.

In the same way as last time, my family met us in Berlin. In Switzerland, the welcome was warmer than the earlier departure. Both sets of grandparents were duly impressed with their grandchildren and happy for our happiness.

At the office of the church headquarters, we officially accepted a call to Shiloh Mission in Northern Transvaal, in the northeast of

South Africa. It was an out-post mission that had been closed for two years. What a challenge! What a joy!

Helen's aptitude for languages and her natural love for human beings of any culture or color eased our work. Every hardship of my past helped us at some point in the next few years. I learned many new things: to drive and main-

On the first visit back to Europe after Georg graduated from Helderberg College, at the end of 1954. Georg's father with Heinz, Helen, and Georg's mother.

tain a car or motorbike that forded rivers and traveled roads and trails more suitable for all-terrain vehicles; to run a filmstrip projec-tor powered by a car battery; to come running when I heard wife or child yell "Snake!"; to build with local materials and methods; to move an evangelistic meeting out under the trees when two hundred people tried to push into a tent that seated one hundred; to start churches and build them up; to find ways to love both blacks and whites in a country that separated them by apartheid; to share God with, and be a brother to, people of the Bantu, Venda, Shangaan, and other tribes.

Helen's deep love fed my soul—no matter how much of my soul I gave to her, it always seemed her love surpassed mine. Our growing boys delighted us too. I was the happiest I had ever been.

Finally, I made it on time for the birth of a child. Helen shook me partially awake at 2:00 A.M. "My water broke," she announced. "It's time to go."

Suddenly I was awake. The last missionaries here, on the way to the hospital to have a baby, had gotten stuck in the river we had to cross. The new father delivered the baby himself. Helen had been through labor and delivery twice. I had been away for both. I was not interested in having my introduction to childbirth to be hands-on.

I jumped out of bed. As prearranged, I telephoned a neighbor to come spend the rest of the night with our boys. The neighbor arrived as I was helping Helen into the old Studebaker.

Driving the twenty miles of dust and washboard in a car of questionable dependability—in the middle of the night, through the bush—I prayed I would *not* be the one attending Helen. The contractions came harder and closer together. I tried to encourage her. I drove as fast as I dared. We made it through the river. As soon as we bounced to a stop in the hospital driveway, I helped Helen into the hospital.

A nurse greeted us and got the particulars. "Just sit here in the waiting room, and I will call the doctor," she said calmly.

"I can't sit anymore," Helen announced, breathing hard.

"You will be fine," the nurse assured as she turned away.

Another contraction hit.

The nurse turned back toward us. "Don't push!" she yelled. "Breathe deep!"

Suddenly, the nurse was moving fast, yelling orders to her assistant. Helen was in the delivery room in moments. I sighed in deep relief. Baby Evelyn arrived before the doctor did. I had never seen a baby so young. I welcomed her, too, with tears of delight and gratitude.

As furlough approached for us after seven years on the front line of mission service, church headquarters asked if we would be willing to help build up the work at Ndora Mission, near the Rwanda-Burundi border. There had been no missionary at the station for several years. We discussed the program, and it sounded interesting.

"There is one thing I must tell you," the union conference president said, with a tone and demeanor that indicated he thought he was going to drop a bomb into our discussion. "The president of the field is a national. You would be his subordinate."

"Yes?" I questioned, expecting the bomb to come next.

"We have not tried having a foreign missionary be subordinate to a national before," he said. "I hope it will work out."

"Why shouldn't it?" I asked. "These people are my brothers and sisters."

Our family decided to accept the call. We sold our furniture and packed other belongings to be shipped to Burundi. Leaving was bittersweet—we bid a tearful goodbye to our loved family surrounding Shiloh Mission then headed to Germany and Switzerland to visit our biological families. Two beautiful reunions awaited us. We enjoyed the visits and hated to leave. Yet, a part of us was also eager to return—Africa was our home. Africa had our hearts.

We returned by driving an Opel Caravan through the beautiful, snowy Alps and south through Italy. We boarded a ship in Naples and sailed to the Suez Canal, where camels pulled the ship. The ship continued down Africa's east coast, and we disembarked at Mombasa, Kenya, and headed for our new assignment—Ndora Mission in Burundi.

We drove the unpaved main highway in Kenya toward the capital city, Nairobi. The dust was so thick it was impossible to pass another vehicle—rather, we avoided a car closer than about two miles, allowing the thick, fine dust time to settle. We needed to be able to see—elephants had the right of way.

We saw Mount Kilimanjaro in the distance. It took several days to get to Lake Victoria—Africa's biggest lake. Then several more days going west and then south across Uganda. We arrived at the Rwanda border late in the afternoon just as the customs office was closing and waited overnight on the concrete floor of the customs building. Since there was political unrest and shooting ahead, the next morning we waited till several cars came that could travel together. When evening came, we enjoyed the hospitality of a Catholic mission. The next day we headed for our church's union headquarters in Bujumbura, Burundi.

Driving through a small village, Helen said, "Look!" She pointed to a sign. "Isn't that our mission?"

"Ndora Mission," I read. "Yes." After this long trip, finding home, wherever it was, seemed enticing. "I wonder how far it is."

"Let's ask," she suggested.

"Did you mean you will ask?" I questioned. "You're the one who speaks some French."

She smiled. "Sure."

I stopped the car as we approached a young man. Helen pointed back to the sign. "How far to Ndora Mission?"

"Ndora," he said. "Uh-h-h, five miles."

"Thank you, sir," Helen responded with a smile.

"Can we go?" three young voices chorused from the back seat.

"Only five miles," I said. I looked at the fuel gauge then at Helen. "We should have enough gasoline to go five miles and back and still make it to Bujumbura."

Travel-weary and eager to see our new home, we headed toward Ndora Mission.

Christmas 1958 in South Africa. Back row: Georg, Helen. Front row: David, Evelyn, Heinz

Helen straightened the children's clothes and combed their hair and hers. We expected after each curve to see the mission.

We drove ten miles. The road was in ill repair, and we crossed makeshift bridges. At the best of times we got up to ten or fifteen miles per hour. Pretty soon we had driven twenty miles. Then twenty-five. The gas gauge was leaning closer to empty.

Smoke rose from huts as women prepared the evening meal. We passed several men carrying spears. I braked. "I'll ask these men," I said.

Fear fell over Helen's face. "No!" she said.

"We don't know where we are, night is approaching, and we are low on gas," I countered. "What choice do we have?"

"Be careful," she pleaded.

I got out of the car and walked toward the four men carrying spears.

They eyed me closely. As I approached, they turned and ran into the bush.

I walked back to the car and climbed in. Even the children were quiet. We drove on. Darkness fell over the bush. We came to a fork in the road. There were no signs.

Should we go right or should we go left?

Brothers
1962

"Dear God," I prayed. "After seven years in Transvaal, I should have known better than to head out into the bush with the amount of gas we had when I wasn't sure how far we would need to go. Please forgive me. Please show us Your grace again. Please send Your angels to keep us safe. And please help us know which way to go."

Both Helen and I sensed we should go right.

We bounced along a few more miles. Suddenly, we came upon a sign: "Ndora Mission." We drove in.

All was quiet. I got out of the car and looked around. A man came out of a house. He looked at me, at the full car, and back at me. "Brother Grellmann?" he asked.

"Yes," I said.

A wide smile broke across his face. "Welcome!" he said, pumping my hand. "Welcome!" He looked into the van. "Welcome to Ndora!" He looked back at me again. "Did the union president tell you where your home is?"

"We haven't seen him yet."

"You haven't?"

"No," I responded. "We saw the sign on the main road, and a man told us it was only five miles. So, we thought we would come on our way to Bujumbura."

"Five miles!" he huffed. "More like thirty-five. I hope you had plenty of fuel."

"I was getting worried," I said. "Especially when we came to the fork three miles back. We didn't have a clue which way we should go."

"So, how did you figure out which way?"

"We prayed."

"Well, praise the Lord you made it here," he bellowed. "The other way, there was a landslide. The road is out, and there are no signs. You could have driven right over a cliff and no one would have heard from you again. I am glad you made it here safely!" He motioned toward my family. "Are you folks hungry?"

"No," I said. "We ate on the way. But I think we are all exhausted. Could we stay the night in the house that will be ours?"

"Certainly!" he said. He led us to our house.

The children ran from room to room. "We're home!" they shouted.

It didn't take long to unpack. We would get by with the barest of necessities until our belongings arrived from Shiloh Mission. For now, we had a lantern and one small kettle. And we had one bowl, one spoon, one cup, and one thin blanket apiece.

The next morning the mission treasurer found some gas for us. It took six hours to drive the narrow, curvy, mountainous road seventy-five miles to Bujumbura. The union officers welcomed us warmly. We discussed our mission. Just before we left, one said, "You are just coming, and we are all leaving."

I must have looked puzzled.

"The celebration of independence is next week. Sometimes it gets violent. Most foreigners leave the country during that time."

And here I am arriving with a wife and three small children! I thought. *Taking them into the bush with no human protection. Why didn't someone tell me about this anniversary when we were making plans?*

Helen and I discussed the situation. "You know," she finally concluded, "God knew about this celebration all along. We've asked for His guidance with every step of planning. Maybe this is an opportunity to let the people know we don't separate ourselves from them. To let them see they truly are our brothers and sisters. Let's stay and trust ourselves to God."

"All right," I agreed. "Let's stay and pray. We'll leave the rest up to God."

We obtained a few supplies in town. Just before we left, I filled both the gas tank and an extra gas can to the brim.

On the way back to our new home, Helen and I talked about our new mission and hoped for a few quiet days to get acclimated to the situation. The trip was tiresome, but at least we knew the way!

The next day, we got word that the king of Burundi and his retinue were making a tour of the country before the celebration of independence. He was encouraging the Hutu and Tutsi people to keep their celebrations peaceful. He would be visiting Ndora Mission the next day. Helen would be expected to feed the royal group a full meal.

"How many are there?" Helen asked.

"About twenty," the messenger replied.

So much for a few quiet days!

After the initial shock, besides praying, Helen went around to the homes of teachers and staff. She enquired what food was available locally and started planning. She borrowed kettles to cook in and gathered food. She borrowed plates, cups, and cutlery. By two o'clock the next afternoon, when the king and his twenty assistants arrived, a feast fit for a king was ready—millet, lentil sauce, flat bread, and platters of fresh vegetables. The meal and the meeting went well.

Lying in bed that evening, I heard rain pound our metal roof. After the downpour, frogs croaked as if excited by the rainstorm. I listened to Helen's soft sleep-breathing beside me. She deserved to sleep! *God, I prayed silently, please give her a sweet, restful sleep tonight.*

As usual, Helen had been a wonderful hostess. She had done a marvelous job of making the little she had into a festive occasion that delighted the king of our new country. Helen loved the people wherever we went, and they loved her in return. She thrived on the rigors of front line mission work. *God,* I prayed silently, *thank You for helping me not to run ahead of You but to wait till You changed Helen's heart. Thank You for giving me a wife who loves this work as much as I do.*

We prayed for safety for Ndora Mission and for ourselves through the anniversary of independence. On our campus, the quiet celebration was totally peaceful.

A couple of days later, our field president arrived. Elder Sembegare was a Hutu from Rwanda—where civil war was tearing the country apart. The Tutsis were in power in Burundi. Elder Sembegare, as custom required, took me to meet the local Tutsi chief. The chief was polite but eyed us suspiciously. I tried to assure him that we at Ndora Mission wanted to help keep peace in his area.

Within days, Tutsi refugees came to our mission. Should we allow them to stay? Elder Sembegare, being a Hutu, thought it better if I made the decision. Though I knew the political situation was tense, I was too new to grasp all the nuances of the decision I was about to make. I sent an S.O.S. heavenward—*God, what do I do?*

I advised that we accept as many of the Tutsi refugees as we were able to accommodate.

Among the Tutsi refugees who stayed was a medical orderly. A small dispensary sat on our campus, unused for some time. I hadn't had time to give any thought to the future of the clinic before a teacher came running. "*Bwana* Grellmann," he cried. "Help! Come help!"

Hutu neighbors of the mission had carried a boy to us. The eight-year-old had fallen from a tree. His forehead was split open, exposing the skull. The swelling was so great we couldn't see his eye on that side.

"Get the orderly!" I directed. "Bring him to the dispensary."

The teacher took off running.

I silently screamed, *Help, God!* and led the entourage to the clinic.

The orderly and I looked the dispensary over for supplies. We found sulfur powder and suture. We didn't find anything to numb pain, or any suturing needle. I sent for one of Helen's sewing needles, then sterilized it over a candle flame—at least I hoped the flame would sterilize it.

I held the needle out to the orderly.

"No, no," he pleaded. "I am Tutsi. He is Hutu." Fear filled the orderly's eyes. "If I sutured and something went wrong, it would not be good!"

Oh, God, I prayed, *please help!*

I sprinkled plenty of amorphous sulfur into the wound, pulled the skin together, and poked the straight needle through the skin on one side of the cut and then the other. Without any anesthetic, the boy lay still on the table. *Help, God!* I pleaded silently. I poked stitch after stitch, pulling the skin together.

We sent the boy home and prayed that the wound would not get infected and would heal well. We prayed often for a good outcome— for the boy, for God's mission.

Daily I became more aware of the tenuous situation near us. But there was nothing we could do about stilling war in the next country, even though the border was close. Our job was to love the people of all types whose lives we touched.

Three weeks after my first surgical experience, the wounded boy returned with his family. He was walking this time. The wound had healed well. He could see out of his eye again.

I pointed up to the sky. "God healed you!" I said. "God helped you to see again. God loves you." We removed the suture and praised God!

A knock came at our house one night. "Missies, missies."

I opened our door.

"Missies," a man begged.

Helen joined me at the door.

"My wife need help to have baby! Missies, come," he said.

There was silence for an instant. "Wait," Helen answered. "I will come." She gathered a few things into a bag and grabbed a hurricane lamp. She gave me a quick kiss at the door. "Pray," she said. "I don't know what I can do. Please pray."

"I will," I promised.

She disappeared with the stranger. I was thankful for her courage. It also tempted me to worry sometimes. I did pray!

"Where's Mama?" the children asked when they got up the next morning.

"She went to help a lady who is having a baby," I told them. "Let's pray for the new mama, for the baby, and for your mama."

Helen arrived home midmorning. "God blessed," she assured us. "The baby lived, and the new mama is fine."

Not many weeks passed till another messenger called, "Missies, missies. Come help!"

Helen saw the handwriting on the wall. She read about labor and delivery and talked to every nurse she had a chance to meet. She packed a small suitcase with needed items so she would always be ready. She loved assisting in labor and delivery and became known in the area as a midwife.

I came to appreciate my superior, Elder Sembegare. He was a very spiritual man who loved his Lord and His people. We worked well together.

Helen and I felt the same way about my superior and about the people we served—it didn't matter whether a person was black or white, Hutu or Tutsi. It didn't matter if their customs were different from ours. If human blood ran through their veins, they were a brother or a sister.

Ndora Mission became known as a place of peace. We had both Tutsi and Hutu on staff and students of both tribes too. Neighbors of both heritages came for help. Leaders of both tribes trusted us with their presence and their questions. We rebuilt more than dormitories and cafeterias. What a thrill on Sabbaths to look out over the congregation—brothers and sisters whom I had taught and who had taught me. People who, if Christ did not dwell in them, would be enemies. But they had received grace, and they extended that grace.

One beautiful day, overlooking the mission that Helen and I loved, I considered what had brought me to this place of peace. Looking back, I saw more clearly than I ever had before that everything God had allowed to come into my life, He had used for good in some way. He had accepted me where I was and loved me into grace—grace I received, grace I could give. There had been challenges before; there would be challenges again. But if we would just let God lead and let Him be in control, His work would move forward.

"Thank You, God," I prayed, "for the peace and purpose You have given me. Thank You for the privilege of being Your emissary in this place. Help me to fail no man . . . No, more than that. Help me always to point my brothers and sisters here to You—the God who will never fail them."

Epilogue

The years flew by happily for Helen and me as we and our growing family continued to serve our brothers and sisters in Africa. Two more babies came along—Dietmar and Reinhold increased the clan to the perfect number of seven.

In addition to working in South Africa's Northern Transvaal and in Burundi, I served as field president from Rwankeri Mission in Northern Rwanda. In our twelve years as missionaries in Africa, our family experienced love, humor, injustice, understanding, huge expectations, miracles, tight budgets, prejudice, and surprises—some delightful, some shocking. We felt great sadness and great joy. We learned to depend more fully on God. We developed practical skills we didn't know we had.

While Georg was field president and the family lived at Rwankeri Mission in Rwanda, where every year there were approximately 1,500 baptisms. Back row: Georg, Reinhold held by Helen. Front row: David, Dietmar, Evelyn, Heinz

We taught and we learned. We loved God, and some whom our lives touched learned to love Him too. We loved people, and many responded in kind. We had our share of tense moments, and many opportunities to work as peacemakers to quiet brewing tensions. We saw atrocities resulting from hate and suspicion; we saw brotherhood among former enemies who had been transformed by the gospel of Jesus Christ.

1967: The family was on their way to Canada. Back row: Evelyn, Heinz, Helen, Georg's mother, Georg, David. Front row: Dietmar, Reinhold

In Africa, I regained objectivity. I learned that happiness does not come from acquiring but comes from serving. I saw that those who are transformed by the gospel of Jesus Christ live with greater joy and higher purpose. I experienced the thrill of promoting education, of building up the work of Christ, of leading people to Jesus.

While in Winnipeg, Manitoba, Canada. Back row: Helen, Heinz, Evelyn, David, Georg. Front row: Reinhold, Dietmar

When Heinz, our oldest child, was ready for high school, our family immigrated to the Canadian province of Manitoba and a few years later to Wisconsin in the United States. I pastored in both areas.

At one point, Helen had a malignant tumor removed. The surgeon felt they had gotten all the cancer. The hardest trial of my life came later when it was discovered that her cancer had returned and metastasized.

Helen made a final trip with Dietmar and Reinhold to see her mother and other family members in Switzerland, scheduling her return so they could be at Evelyn's graduation from Canadian Union Academy in Alberta. As a surprise for Helen, I arranged for the older boys to come too. Together, Heinz, David, Evelyn, and I met Helen and the younger boys at the Edmonton, Alberta, airport.

As Helen came off the plane she was using crutches to support herself. The expression on her face when she saw us all was priceless.

Back row: Georg, Helen, Jo's wife, Jo. Front row: Georg's mother and father

As we reached the car, one of the children pointed to the sky and gasped, "Look!"

Sun burst through the clouds. Helen gazed at the rays streaming earthward. Then she looked around at all of us. "That's how I imagine it will be when Jesus comes," she said, "all of us together again."

The days after Helen's death were dark for me. I prayed for strength. Already tired from caring for Helen as best I could, I did my best to pastor and care for my ten- and twelve-year-old sons. I tried to be strong, but at night after my boys were asleep, I laid my broken heart bare before God.

As difficult and painful and lonely as those days were, my heart was strangely strengthened by my God. Through the worst of Helen's pain, God strengthened and encouraged her. She held on to His hand, His peace, His joy. Through the worst of my days, He held me up also. He didn't give me every answer—many will have to wait till eternity. But He gave me strength to open my eyes to each new day, strength to progressively trust the unanswered questions to Him. He gave me a peace that was deeper than the pain. I have tested God. Truly, He does not fail.

Mr. Schaeffer, whose home I stayed in some weekends in Germany as a teen while I was in the Youth Work Camp, had lost his wife during the war and immigrated to the United States. My parents had stayed in contact with him through the years, and he contacted me after hearing of my sorrow. Eventually, he told me

about the joy his second wife had brought to him and suggested that when I was ready to consider another woman, he and his wife knew two, but Charleene was their first choice.

2002: Fiftieth anniversary celebration of Seventh-day Adventist churches in Vendaland, in the north of South Africa, next to Kruger National Park. Georg and Pastor Mkasi started the church there fifty years before with eight members. Now 2,500 members attend several churches.

Eventually I was ready. Charleene was a special woman who had the courage to come into our family. She has brought much joy to me and the children. I continued then to pastor—in the states of Illinois and Washington—and Charleene served the children and our churches well.

2004 family reunion at Priest Lake, Idaho, U.S.A. Charleene and Georg with five children and their spouses, and twelve grandchildren

I have loved all of my churches, but a part of my heart remains in Africa. It was a special thrill recently to be invited to a fiftieth-anniversary celebration of churches in Vendaland, South Africa. Pastor Mack Mkasi and I started the work among the smaller tribe of Vendas that borders Krueger National Park. We established the first church with eight members. Now, twenty-five hundred believers fill several churches.

Not long before I retired from the pastorate, one of my members asked me to visit a man whose doctors had informed that he had two weeks to live. "But be careful," my parishioner added. "He doesn't like ministers."

When I visited the man in his home, he sat, leaning against the elevated head of a hospital bed. It didn't take long to figure out that he was quite a character. He seemed to be used to being the one in charge, to making things happen the way he wanted.

After we talked a bit, I said, "They tell me you are nearing the end of your life. Have you made provision for your children?"

"Yes," he answered with characteristic brusqueness.

"Have you made provision for your wife?"

"Yes."

"What about Him?" I pointed and looked upward.

The dying man leaned forward till his reddening face was close to mine. "I am not a sinner!" he snapped.

I was shocked. No one had ever told me that. I sent God another silent S.O.S. *Help!*

I moved my face a little closer to the man's, looking him straight in the eye. I shrugged my shoulders. "Well, then—" the words just seemed to tumble out of my mouth, "you don't have to worry about any of this that the doctors say. Only sinners die."

Georg's five children—Reinhold, Dietmar, Evelyn, David, Heinz. In birth order, their professions are engineer, physician, speech therapist, attorney, and engineer. All five have worked abroad, four as missionaries.

The man blinked slowly but didn't avert his gaze. The room was silent. "Well," he finally started, a new softness edging his voice, "what should I do?"

"I'd recommend you read the Gospels," I said.

The man relaxed back against the head of his bed.

After a fairly lengthy silence, I asked, "Do you have a Bible?"

"Yes, sir," he said. "I'm sure there's one around here."

Often in the next days I prayed that this harsh man would read and that he would see the Savior clearly.

A few days later, I stopped by his house again. The man was sitting in bed again, this time with the Bible on his lap and a totally different expression on his face. His eyes lighted up when he saw me. "I've been reading," he said with a smile.

"What do you think of it?" I asked.

"It's different than I thought religion was," he said. He asked a few questions and thanked me for stopping by. "I'm almost through Matthew," he said. "I'm going to keep reading."

I visited several times. One day his smile was especially big. "I asked Jesus to forgive me," he said. "I've never felt such peace."

About a week later, he died. His friend told me he was totally peaceful.

I was grateful this man found peace before he died but sad that he had missed so much life by accepting the Savior so late. I have tried my God. I know His promise is true—He came to give life that is abundant! Overflowing. Life with Him, life serving Him and my fellow humans has filled my life with purpose, peace, and joy.

In times of war, God alone can give us peace. Here are more amazing war stories.

Rainbow Over Hell

Tsuneyuki Mohri translated by Sharon Fujimoto-Johnson

Perhaps it was destiny, but time and again, Saburo faced imminent death—and barely escaped. Easily one of the most dramatic conversion stories you'll ever read, Rainbow Over Hell lets you see the horrors of World War II through the eyes of a Japanese youth who joined the resistance against the Americans and became an assassin. Saburo's eventual arrest and death sentence formed the backdrop for a life-altering encounter with another condemned Man who died long ago to secure his freedom.

Paperback, 192 pages   0-8163-2134-5   US$14.99

Shot Down

John M. Curnow

After his bomber exploded, author John Curnow found himself riding a parachute down to German-occupied France—his crew's sole survivor. Read this book and you'll know how it felt to look down the muzzle of an enemy's rifle. And you'll know how John felt when he found his way to true freedom in Christ.

Paperback, 222 pages   0-8163-2109-4   US$15.99

Whom Shall I Fear?

Ann Vitrovich

Spanning two world wars, this is the incredible true story of one courageous woman. For Mara, life was a war zone, from battle-scarred Serbia in World War I to World War II. In between, Mara met Jesus and trusted Him with her life. Could her faith sustain her family in their darkest hour?

Paperback, 144 pages   0-8163-2129-9   US$12.99

Order from your ABC by calling **1-800-765-6955**, or get online and shop our virtual store at **http://www.AdventistBookCenter.com**.

• Read a chapter from your favorite book
• Order online
• Sign up for e-mail notices on new products

Prices subject to change without notice.